PRAISE GOD AND THANK HIM

PRAISE GOD
AND
THANK HIM

Biblical Keys for a Joyful Life

JEFF CAVINS

PUBLISHED BY FRANCISCAN MEDIA
Cincinnati, Ohio

Cover design by LUCAS Art & Design, Jenison, Michigan
Cover image © Masterfile
Book design by Mark Sullivan

LIBRARY OF CONGRESS CATALOGING-IN-PUBLICATION DATA
Cavins, Jeff.
Praise God and thank him : biblical keys for a joyful life / by Jeff Cavins.
pages cm
ISBN 978-1-61636-723-7 (alk. paper)
1. Praise of God—Biblical teaching. 2. Gratitude—Biblical teaching. I. Title.
BS680.P63C38 2014
248.3—dc23
2014002139
ISBN 978-1-61636-723-7

Published by Servant Books, an imprint of Franciscan Media.
28 W. Liberty St.
Cincinnati, OH 45202
www.FranciscanMedia.org

Printed in the United States of America.
Printed on acid-free paper.
14 15 16 17 18 5 4 3 2 1

Contents

F o r e w o r d

—————⬭⬭⬭—————

It puzzled and confounded all the greatest artistic minds of the day. For years the block of marble was surveyed yet left untouched by every sculptor who examined the mammoth rock. Nearly four decades went by as the gorgeous marble slab sat unused, occupying space in the back lot of the cathedral in Florence. The problem, you ask? It wasn't the height, standing about eighteen feet tall, nor the size, weighing in at well over six tons. No, the problem stemmed from the fact that the last artist who'd attempted to sculpt the marble left a hole running all the way through it when he was forced to cease his work. None of the artists that followed could figure out how to work with such a profound imperfection.

It wasn't until 1501 when the great Michelangelo Buonarroti gazed upon the giant slab that the marble would find its true purpose: to become the great statue of David. Michelangelo would slay the giant marble by unearthing from it the great giant-slayer.

Michelangelo perceived something that other minds—even brilliant and gifted minds—failed to see. He deduced that by tilting and turning the stone to a very precise angle, he could carve around the hole. In the hands of a master, the perceived problem, which rendered the marble seemingly useless, became part of the solution in a masterpiece. Others saw the flawed stone; Michelangelo saw the stone slinger. Some quote Michelangelo as having said, "I saw the angel in the marble and carved until I set him free."

It takes more than working knowledge of a chisel for a sculptor to unearth a masterpiece. A sculptor only becomes a true artist when blessed with perspective. It's with that distinction in mind that I am so grateful to pen a foreword to this book, written—and more to the point, *crafted*—by a true artist, mentor, and friend, Jeff Cavins.

On the pages to follow Jeff is going to do far more than give you a new book to keep at your bedside. In this book Jeff is giving you a priceless treasure, a pearl of great price, a gift for you and your family today that *must* become a family heirloom for years to come: the gift of *perspective.*

Perspective is a fascinating word, etymologically speaking. From the Latin, perspective comes from two words: *per* (meaning "through") and *specere* (meaning "to look"). So, quite literally, having the proper *perspective* is not as much about looking *at* a situation as it is about looking *through* a situation. God specializes in helping his children capture or regain perspective, if their hearts are humble and trusting enough to let him do so.

The Israelites saw the Red Sea, but God and (soon) Moses saw a path through it. Saul's army saw an unconquerable Philistine warrior, but God and (soon) David saw arrogance and blasphemy. Simeon foresaw great sufferings, but God and Mary knew well that suffering would be the path to salvation. You may look at your current situation—your marriage or family, job or debt, addiction or temptations, health or future—as hopeless or impossible, but God can work with those "holes"; the master Potter (Isaiah 64:8) is also a master sculptor who can chisel away your rough edges. God knows and soon you (through the help in this book) will trust that his almighty hand is working away to make all things new in you. Regardless of your personal situation or daily cross (see Luke 9:23), this book will give you practical steps to take next. In short, the sooner you praise and thank God for each breath—no matter your challenges—the sooner you'll be breathing easier. Prayer alters perspective. Scripture widens our gaze.

Many perceive the Bible merely as pithy advice for moral living, but as any passionate believer knows, it's so much more. The Bible is more than insight on how to live, it's an invitation to die—to yourself and to this world—as we collectively seek and strive for eternal life in heaven.

The Bible is an invitation to live through a challenge to die. God's Word calls us to surrender. The path to surrender does not end with praise, as you'll find out, but praise and thanksgiving are the first, most important yet oft-forgotten steps. When you begin to view the stories of Scripture and your personal stories through this lens of praise and thanksgiving, things change. Your life's mountains can become molehills in the blink of an eye, the opening of your heart, and the turn of each page.

Consider your Bible a treasure chest, filled with priceless truths and wisdom. This book provides you with the key to access all of them in their fullness. Within each story and throughout every chapter, you'll be reintroduced to familiar figures and timeless stories from Sacred Scripture. As each story is retold and reframed, however, you will begin to see a pattern occur. What did God's children then know that many of his children now seem to forget? Jeff submits that it's the power of praise and the thoughtfulness to thank God—and I couldn't agree more.

We all have giants in our lives that seem insurmountable. David had one, literally (as you'll hear about in chapter four). How many of us, though, just reactively grab a sword and charge ahead or grab a shield and run away? How many of us when staring down the giants in life have the courage not only to pray for deliverance but also praise God in assurance of victory?

In this book, God comes to us, yet again, through words about His Word. While we must never spend more time reading books *about* sacred Scripture than we spend reading the Word of God, itself, we ought to offer God thanks for works such as this one, which should be carried in tandem with our Bible. The words that follow will guide and beckon you ever deeper into the inexhaustible, scriptural ocean of God's grace.

How do we make praise more practical in our busy daily lives? How do we learn to thank God more readily and steadily throughout the sun *and the storms*? What is the Holy Spirit trying to reveal to us through His Word, and what can we learn from the legacies of our ancestors in the faith? Prepare to have your questions answered, your heart touched, your worries relieved, and your soul stirred.

I'm offering praise and thanksgiving to God for the gift of this book, as I'm sure you will soon be doing, too.

Let our Father, the master sculptor, use this book and its author to chisel and hone us in our daily faith walks, while revealing and unleashing God's greatness to a world desperately in need of it. Incidentally, if you follow the steps laid out in this book, you'll probably become a saint—which just could lead to you having a statue sculpted one day. How's that for irony?

Michelangelo saw greatness in a flawed rock. Imagine how much more greatness the Father sees in us living stones! Praise and thank God that he sees more in us than we see in ourselves.

All God needs to make a masterpiece in you is your consent. Turning the page gives it. Go ahead—I dare you.

—Mark Hart

As the years have passed, I have had the opportunity to see how praising and thanking God can make a difference in my life and in the lives of others. Over the years while serving in various ministries, I have heard from many people about the obstacles they face in everyday life. One common question centers on what to do when things look impossible. In my quest to find answers for my life and also to encourage others, I began to study the Scriptures to find some solutions. It did not take long before I noticed that people in the Bible had no problem complaining to God about their problems, just like so many of us, but then, after they did their complaining, often they began to praise God for his greatness and thank him for the mighty deeds he had done.

I learned from Moses that the Lord answered praise and thanksgiving with great deliverance. Gideon, Samson, David, Ezra, Nehemiah, Paul, Peter—they all had lessons to learn about what to do when times got tough, desperate, or impossible.

As time progressed in the Bible, each person would recall the great deeds of the Lord, so by the time of Paul there was an incredible amount of evidence chronicling the faithfulness of the Lord. Now, after two thousand years, today we have so much to draw from when we find ourselves wondering if God cares about our situation. We'll be looking at many of these Bible greats and what they had to say about praise and thanksgiving in future chapters.

So what about *your* battles? What are you facing today that looks impossible? One of the things that defeats many of us from the very start is that we are inspired by the stories in the Bible but cannot see ourselves responding the way the Bible characters did. We look around and we don't see God interacting in our situations the same way he did with Moses or Abraham or King David. Did God only answer those who lived in biblical times, or does he still intervene in people's lives today? Can God turn around situations that make you feel penned in on every side? The answer is a resounding yes! In fact, the prophet Zechariah said to the remnant of Judah trying to rebuild their nation and Temple that God's involvement, his power, is key when facing difficult situations.

> Then he said to me, "This is the word of the LORD to Zerubbabel: Not by might, nor by power, but by my Spirit, says the LORD of hosts." (Zechariah 4:6)

The pattern in Scripture is consistent. When faced with difficulty, people responded in a specific way for success. To be victorious, they responded with praise.

Hebrews 13:8 tells us that Jesus Christ is the same yesterday, today, and forever. What if God still enters into the life of his people and rescues them and delivers them from all their enemies? What about *your* difficult situation? A powerful question to ask yourself is this: "Does God still stand with his people and move mightily in their lives?" If he doesn't, then all the knowledge of God you might gain from studying the Bible, all knowledge of Church history and Church teaching, will merely leave you with great ideas and pithy sayings. Without God's presence here and now in your life, your faith will be void of any power or substance to actually change your circumstances and your own thinking.

Back in the 1970s, Merlin Carothers wrote a book called *Power in Praise*. He used the example of driving a car without power steering (remember those days?). Without power steering, the steering wheel is hard to turn, but with it, it's a breeze. Carothers compared this to praising vs. complaining. He said praise is like power steering—once you begin to praise, things get easier. But if you just sit and complain, everything is harder. The way to begin is to just step out and trust God.

The Church has given us the gift of the saints' lives to encourage us that in every generation, God does great things in people's lives. But does that mean you have to be a saint in order for God to help you in your time of need? Remember, the saints were all ordinary people too at one time. They needed to call on the Lord for help, just like you and me. St. Augustine said our hearts are restless unless they rest in God. This restlessness often accompanies the great challenges in our lives. By actively praising God and giving him thanks, our hearts will find the resting place that we so desire. St. Teresa of Avila said this:

> Let nothing disturb you,
> Let nothing frighten you.
> All things are passing away:
> God never changes.[1]

There Will Always Be Problems

One thing is certain: Life will never be problem free. Look at what happens in the world on any given week—wars, terrorist attacks, government shutdowns, natural disasters, horrific accidents, violent crime, and high unemployment rates. Individuals are faced with job loss, serious illness, and family tragedies. Problems are a fact of life.

When people are faced with obstacles or problems, they might respond positively, or they might respond negatively, or they might choose to do nothing. But they *will* respond. Some deny that the problem exists. Others run away from their problems. Still others look for someone else to blame. In the Bible there are those who chose to respond positively to devastating situations: Job is just one example. There are also examples of those who responded negatively to their situations: King Saul, or Judas, for instance. We'll look at them in more detail in the first section of the book.

Therefore, it's important to realize that it's not a question of *if* we are going to respond, but *how* we respond to our problems and obstacles that will determine whether we are successful in our walk with God or whether we will become even more frustrated with the difficulties that we face.

THE BEST RESPONSE

There are plenty of inferior ways to respond to problems and handle the stress in your life. You can respond by yelling or by throwing something. You might turn to alcohol or become addicted to social media and the Internet. But how would you like to learn a new way of dealing with the difficulties in your life? How would you like to learn God's prescribed way of dealing with difficulties—praise and thanksgiving? Wouldn't it be valuable to learn to respond to difficulties in a way that changes both you and your circumstances? That's what this book is all about.

The answer to the question of whether God still moves mightily in the lives of his people is overwhelmingly yes. God never changes. God wants to move in your life. But in order for him to act in your life, some things are required of you. First and foremost is your cooperation. The prophet Hosea said,

Sow for yourselves righteousness,
reap the fruit of steadfast love;
break up your fallow ground,
for it is the time to seek the LORD,
that he may come and rain salvation upon you. (Hosea 10:12)

You'll need to learn about God and his ways. It also will require a harnessing of your will so you can turn your life and your circumstances over to God—even when everything looks dark and you feel like you are on the brink of despair. Breaking up the fallow ground of habits and patterns will be necessary to walk in the victory God wants to give you.

IF YOU FEEL HOPELESS...

Before we go any further, let me extend an anchor of hope to you if you feel hopeless. Not only can your perspective change in terms of how you are viewing your present circumstances, but those circumstances can change, too. There is always hope! Maybe you are facing a personal crisis in your marriage, at work, or in the life of one of your children. Perhaps you or someone close to you is struggling with a health issue, a financial challenge, relationship problems, or job security. No matter what the difficulty is, know this: God is with you and wants to be active in the details of your life. He knows your situation and wants to go through it with you. He doesn't want you to go through it alone.

God has something greater than the answers you hear in the world. Today, on television, radio, print media, and the Internet, we are faced with a plethora of life coaches, mentors, pop psychologists, all purporting to solve our challenges and bring us peace and prosperity. Too often, though, all of these various experts lack the power to follow through on their own advice. In the end, they offer simplistic solutions to complex problems. Can a TV host really untie the knots of twenty years of bad behavior in forty minutes? Listening and watching, we feel like we have discovered the secret, and we're ready to move on—only to face the fact that we lack the power to carry out the changes that are necessary. Too many times we come away feeling empowered, only to find out that we actually don't have sufficient power within ourselves to overcome the challenges we're confronted with.

What if there was someone smarter than these authorities? What if there was someone more powerful than the authors of the most popular books in the world today? Someone who knew you so intimately that they knew all your fears, all your weaknesses, and all your strengths? And what if that someone was inviting you to a personal relationship? That someone is God.

This book is about living with God in the challenges of life and discovering a new way to confront obstacles. It's about relearning old habits and taking on the yoke of Jesus—his worldview. It's about following God through the storms and resting in him when the winds blow. It's about confronting our limitations and celebrating God's limitless power.

Praise is creating space in your life for God to do what you are hoping and dreaming he will do. Always remember: With God, nothing is impossible. All things are possible!

PART ONE

Biblical
Praise

Chapter One

BIBLICAL CYCLES:
INSTRUCTION FOR LIVING

This is my God, and I will praise him,
my father's God, and I will exalt him.

—EXODUS 15:2

MANY OF THE GREAT STORIES OF DELIVERANCE WE LEARNED
as children are found in the Old Testament—stories like those of
Noah, David and Goliath, or Gideon and Samson. It is important
to understand that these stories are not fantastical retellings of
mythical characters in incredible circumstances—they are stories
of real people facing real problems in real life. The apostle Paul
said that these things were written for our encouragement:

> For whatever was written in former days was written for
> our instruction, that by steadfastness and by the encour-
> agement of the scriptures we might have hope. (Romans
> 15:4)

We can think of sacred Scripture as the playbook of life, showing
us how we should respond to God in difficult times. It reveals

God's will and his character and shows us how the kingdom of God works. And while many of the stories in the Bible are dramatic and enthralling, they are not meant primarily for our entertainment—they are meant to provide instruction for living.

From the beginning of the Bible to the end, if we look, we can see cyclical patterns. In Genesis 3, for example, we read about the ordeal Adam and Eve faced with the enemy in the Garden of Eden. We see that pattern repeated in the lives of other Bible characters such as Jacob, the nation of Israel, and ultimately Jesus's ordeal in another garden. Not only are these patterns obvious when reading the Bible, they also teach us the proper response to various predicaments.

EXILE AND RETURN

We see this cycle of being exiled and then returning repeated over and over in the Bible with individuals as well as the nation of Israel dealing with their enemies. The choice is always whether an individual or nation will choose to look to themselves and their own power and focus only on their own interests, or whether they turn to God and look to him for deliverance. We see this pattern repeatedly—from the Garden of Eden to the land of Canaan. While some did respond correctly to their dilemma, as David did with Goliath, oftentimes they did not, like the children of Israel at Mount Sinai.

But when we come to the New Testament, we see how Jesus is the fulfillment of all of this. He shows us how to respond and how to live; his life is a reenactment of the life of Israel. In other words, in his short human life on earth, he faced what Israel faced. Israel was the firstborn son among all the nations and often failed to keep their covenant with God, but Jesus, God's only begotten Son, never failed. He always responded properly.

An example of this is the repetitive combination of the number three and the desert. Israel spent forty years in the desert and failed three times in their response to God (see Deuteronomy 6–8). Jesus, however, was successful in his three trials in the desert (see Matthew 4). From this repeated cycle we see both the wrong way to respond in stress and the correct way in Christ. A good question to always ask in Bible study is, "How has Christ fulfilled this passage?"

This is important for you to understand, because the combination of looking at failure and success in the Bible will aid you in your own understanding of what constitutes a proper response versus an improper one. We are meant to learn from both the mistakes and successes of the Old Testament, and we certainly can learn from the supreme success of Jesus Christ. Because of this, you do not need to be discouraged about your own past failures; they are not a total waste. You can learn from them, and you can build on them as you begin to learn the proper way to respond in difficult times. For instance, you might be tempted to think in a particular situation, *Well, I have messed up royally.* However, the Israelites messed up royally too, but God was not done with them. The good news is that God is not done with you either.

At a certain point in my life, I had been really struggling with something, and I went to confession. I told the priest about my struggle, and I said something like, "I just wish God would give me one more chance." From the other side of the screen, I remember the priest saying, "The Lord is saying to you, 'Just give *me* one more chance.'" It was an entirely new perspective for me, and very freeing.

And that's what God is saying to you, too. "Just give me one more chance. I can do things in your life that you think are impossible. I know this situation better than you do, and I know you. Just cooperate with me, and we will do this together. You are my child, and I am your God. Let me show you who I am—let me demonstrate my strength in your life. Allow me to guide you with my wisdom. Let me show you how when others failed, my Son was successful."

Jeremiah said it so well: "For I know the plans I have for you, says the LORD, plans for your welfare and not for evil, to give you a future and a hope" (Jeremiah 29:11).

THE SIN CYCLE

In the book of Judges, we can see a recurring pattern when difficulties arose for the Israelites. First they fell into sin, which led to servitude, becoming servants of neighboring nations. Once they grew tired of serving other nations, they moved to supplication, crying out to God for help. Israel's supplication involved first praising God for who he was and what he'd done in the past and then crying out to him for deliverance. God always heard their cries, and he always came to their aid, bringing them salvation and victory. He brought them deliverers like Gideon, Deborah, and Samson, and he delivered them from their enemy. After that, they would enter into a period of silence and peace. This cycle—sin, servitude, supplication, salvation, and silence—was repeated many times. We all long for peace, but we also experience similar cycles. Just when we think life is great, some new problem seems to crop up. Sometimes it's due to sin, sometimes not.

FIRST RESPONDER

The book of Judges poses a key question for us when faced with situations like this. This question is asked two times—first in Judges 1:1 and second in Judges 20:18. The question is this: "Who shall go up first for us to do battle?" In the midst of two different desperate situations, they ask the same question—"In the midst of this battle that we are facing right now, who will go up first in battle?" The Israelites wanted to know which of the twelve tribes of Israel would go up first. The same is true of our lives. When faced with battles, something will go up first. That something tends to be a pattern; we tend to respond to problems the same way. We usually learn how to respond from our parents, and it simply becomes a part of our being; it's the way we handle stress.

So, in the midst of distressing battles in your life, what happens first? Is it the raised voice? Is it throwing something across the room? Is it blaming someone else? Is it drinking? What goes up first? Is it slamming the door and driving off in a rage? What happens first?

In the book of Judges, Judah was the tribe designated to go up first. God answered the Israelites, saying, "Judah shall go up first." Why Judah? I'm sure there are many nuggets to glean from the fact that Judah is the tribe Jesus came from. Revelation 5:5 calls him "the lion of the tribe of Judah." Judah also was the largest tribe. And to the Israelites, the answer might have been even clearer. The answer may have been found in the meaning of the word *Judah* (*Yehuda* in Hebrew)—which means "praised." Therefore, when the Israelites asked the Lord who should go up first, God basically told them that the tribe whose name meant "praise" should go first.

While Judah going into battle first was physically true, it's also metaphorically true that when we are faced with difficulties and enemies all around, our first response should be to praise God. The word *Judah* comes from the root word *yadah*. That root word means "to throw" or "to cast." When this root word is used in other grammatical tenses, it takes on additional meanings of "to confess" or "to declare" something, "to give thanks, laud, or praise." It can mean also to "extend the hands," as in a physical expression of praise. When we praise God, in one sense we are "throwing out" or "casting" a declaration, a confession.

A job loss. An unwanted report from the doctor's office. A teenager in trouble with the law. Facing foreclosure. Eventually everyone is hit by bad news of one kind or another. But the real question is: How will we respond? What do you cast? What do you confess? If we've already developed the habit of praising God, it will be easier to declare his praise. Instead, too often we make these kinds of declarations:

"Oh, woe is me!"

"What a failure I am!"

"Things like this always happen to me."

"I'm such a loser."

"I never get a break."

Remember the answer God gave Israel: "Let Judah [*praise*] go up first." That's our cue as to what we should do when we are faced with our own enemies. When we get the call from the principal or the tax attorney or the doctor, what is our first response? Do we throw up our hands in despair? Do we blame someone else or bemoan what we should have done instead or—worst of all—take it out on those around us? None of these responses help the situation.

Maybe we learned behavior patterns of anger, criticism, or blame from our parents, but it's time for a new response: turning to God with praise. It takes discipline to change our old habits, but with courage and God's grace, praise works! It may not change the situation right away, but it will change you!

The next time you're in defeat or in despair, remember that your trust is in Jesus. Where others failed, he has succeeded.

THE IMPORTANCE OF CONFESSION

In the context of prayer, *yadah*, the root word of Judah, retains the meaning of confession. However, in addition to confessing God's attributes, it also means the confession of our sins to God. This brings a new dimension to praise and worship. Not only do we confess who God is in a particular situation, but we confess our sins to him also. If we are struggling with sin in our lives, we are encumbered and entangled and unable to run the race set before us (see Hebrews 12:1). We certainly do not need to face the problems in our lives with any additional burdens. We won't be successful in battle if we are crippled by sin.

All sin has a negative effect in our lives, because all sin is an offense against God. The Church tells us that there are two kinds of sin: venial sin and mortal sin. The *Catechism of the Catholic Church* has this to say about these two kinds of sin:

> *Mortal sin* destroys charity in the heart of man by a grave violation of God's law; it turns man away from God, who is his ultimate end and his beatitude, by preferring an inferior good to him.

Venial sin allows charity to subsist, even though it offends and wounds it. (CCC 1855)

Venial sin weakens our relationship with God, while mortal sin breaks that relationship with God. Going into a battle weakened or broken is not the optimal choice, is it? Psalm 79:8–9 contains the idea of both confessing our sin and declaring who God is (which is a key element of praise):

> Do not remember against us the iniquities of our forefathers;
>> let thy compassion come speedily to meet us,
>> for we are brought very low.
> Help us, O God of our salvation,
>> for the glory of thy name;
> deliver us, and forgive our sins,
>> for thy name's sake! (Psalm 79:8–9)

Confession and praise go hand in hand. When we confess our sin, we walk in humility. Humility is the proper assessment of who we are in relationship to one another and God. Confessing our sin removes footholds for the enemy to penetrate our lives. A proper assessment of our sin should remind us that we are in need of God's saving work in every area of our lives. Since we are so dependent upon God to free us from sin it should not come as a surprise that we are dependent upon him to assist us in life's battles.

KEY TAKEAWAYS
- The Bible is our playbook, meant to provide us with both instruction and encouragement.

- Just like the Israelites, we tend to respond to situations in our lives according to repetitive patterns.
- Confession and praise go hand in hand.
- Praising God teaches us new ways of responding to life's tough times.

QUESTIONS FOR REFLECTION

1. When you are faced with a tough situation, what is your *first* response? What do you confess?
2. Instead of declaring, "I'm such a failure," how could praising God and declaring who he is change the outcome of a less-than-ideal situation?
3. List some ways that the sacrament of confession has strengthened you in times of trial.

C h a p t e r   T w o

BIBLICAL PRAISE:
KNOWING GOD AND HIS WORKS

O LORD, our Lord,
how majestic is thy name in all the earth!

—PSALM 8:1

THE CATECHISM TELLS US THAT A PERSON DISCLOSES HIMSELF in his actions, and so the better we know a person, the better we understand his or her actions (CCC 236). Before we can praise God in an appropriate way, there are two things we need to know. The *Catechism* outlines these two aspects in that same paragraph.

> The Fathers of the Church distinguish between theology (*theologia*) and economy (*oikonomia*). "Theology" refers to the mystery of God's inmost life within the Blessed Trinity and "economy" to all the works by which God reveals himself and communicates his life. Through the *oikonomia* the *theologia* is revealed to us; but conversely, the *theologia* illuminates the whole *oikonomia*. God's works reveal who he is in himself; the mystery of his inmost being enlightens our understanding of all his works. (CCC 236)

How to Get to Know God Better

Let's look at these two very important ways of knowing God: theology and economy.

Theology refers to the mystery of God's inmost life. Another way of putting this is theology speaks of the heart of God, our heavenly Father, his Son Jesus Christ, and the Holy Spirit. Without an understanding of the Trinity (theology), you'll find yourself compromised in terms of praising God and having the confidence in him in the midst of your difficulties. How can you praise a God that you don't know? How can you have confidence that God will intervene in your life if he's just a distant being to you—if you don't really know him?

By contrast, a person that has an effective life of praise when facing difficult situations is a person who is cultivating a personal relationship with God. This person studies God's Word, reads the *Catechism*, goes to Mass as often as possible, goes to confession regularly, is familiar with the saints, and spends time in prayer with God getting to know his heart. This person talks to God, and God talks to him or her. That's theology.

There is no shortcut to a deep meaningful relationship with another person. Just as a newly married couple must spend hours, days, and years with each other if they are going to hope to really know each other, so the Christian must spend lots of time interacting with God, listening and speaking to him. This notion of generous amounts of time together was at the heart of the rabbi-disciple relationship in Jesus's day. As the disciple (*talmid*) followed, observed, listened to, and talked with the rabbi, he would come to know the heart, worldview, and the temperament of the one he admired. Understanding the heart of God cannot be taught in the objective; it is a relationship. As Jesus said, "Come, follow me" (Matthew 4:19, *NIV*).

Very closely related to knowing the heart of God (theology) is knowing the deeds of God. The *Catechism* defines the second way of coming to know God as the *oikonomia*, where we get the English word *economy*. The economy refers to God's *works*—the way he reveals himself and communicates his life. In order to praise God appropriately, you must know his deeds. By reading the Old Testament and observing his works, you come to know something of the heart of God.

By the way, in modern times we think of economy as relating to money, Wall Street, budget reports, and the state of our nation's economic health. But this word originally was tied to the idea of a father's household plan. So we can look at economy as God's deeds and actions; we're meant to know our Father's family plans. When we know God's deeds, we learn how he will respond in any situation.

We come to know his deeds by immersing ourselves in sacred Scripture. Whether reading the story of David and Goliath, Samson and the Philistines, or Moses at Mt. Sinai, we begin to see more clearly the heart of God. The *Catechism* goes on to say that once we know God's deeds, we begin to know his heart. Conversely, knowing his heart illuminates the understanding of his deeds. In other words, by knowing the heart of God through prayer and study, we come to know his plan, too. This is actually a very powerful thought: We can know the plan of God and the heart behind the plan. Paul put it this way when he wrote to the Corinthians, who were immersed in a pagan culture, "For 'who has known the mind of the Lord so as to instruct him?' But we have the mind of Christ" (1 Corinthians 2:16). In other words, we have some understanding as to how God thinks. Now, *that* is valuable in tough situations!

With this insight from the *Catechism* we can see that the foundation of praising God is *knowing* him—and his works. Securing that foundation today prepares you for difficult times tomorrow. You don't want to wait until some calamity comes upon you to discover that you don't really know God. Of course, if you find yourself in a sticky situation, it's never too late to start learning about God—that's what this book is about. We turn to God in difficult times, and we come to know him better through those difficulties. But if times are great right now, and you're sitting on your deck, drinking an iced tea, and reading your Bible, now is the time to deepen your knowledge of God.

BIBLICAL PRAISE HAS SUBSTANCE

To illustrate how important it is to know the theology (heart of the Trinity) and the economy (the deeds of God), I have contrived this little scenario. Let's say there's an auditorium filled with a thousand people, and it's my job to introduce someone very special. I'm hoping that the audience will give him the proper welcome. I even tell them that upon the completion of the introduction I want them to stand and give him a standing ovation followed by praise of all kinds. I finally say, "Ladies and gentlemen, it's my pleasure to introduce to you today...Mr. John Q. Public." When John Q. Public arrives, the audience, in keeping with my instructions, gives John a standing ovation, followed by exuberant shouts of, "Praise you, John! We praise you, John! Hallelujah! Glory to John Q!"

But within a couple of minutes an inevitable question begins to arise in the hearts of the once-exuberant audience: *Why are we doing this? Why in the world are we praising this guy?* If you were sitting in that audience, you would ask two obvious questions: "Who *is* John Q. Public?" and, "What has he done to deserve my praise?"

Those are the two questions that the *Catechism* answers in paragraph 236. *Who is this Jesus? Why am I praising him? What has he done?* Knowing the answers to these questions constitutes the content of praise. "Lord, I praise you because you are so faithful, and you have never let your people down. You are the one who created the stars and the moon. You created this earth. You defeated the Philistines through the hands of Samson. You are the one that took care of the lion and bear on behalf of a young David. You are the one that came into this world in the midst of darkness and despair and defeated sin, death, and hell. You stood against the devil when he tried to tempt you, and you defeated him with your word."

This is the substance of praise—it's so much more than empty accolades. True biblical praise is infused with the knowledge of who God is as well as a familiarity concerning his deeds. We praise him because we know him; we have a sense of what he will do. This kind of praise declares who God is, what he has done in the past, and our confidence in him today.

Back to John Q. Public. Without any knowledge of who he is and what he has done, praising him is simply a hollow exercise. Now think about yourself. Is your praise life a hollow exercise? Is your praise life void of knowing who God is and what he has done? Is your knowledge of God about as deep and wide as your knowledge of John Q. Public?

"You Are Merciful to All, for You Can Do All Things"

In the Middle Ages, many people were negatively affected by a philosophy called *nominalism*. *Nominialism* is the theory that universal ideas, such as truth, kindness, and God, are only names. It denies that universals, which are things that are true at all times and all places, are true concepts in themselves and are related to and are founded on objective reality. Abstract ideas, according to nominalism, are merely useful labels, subject to change. With this in mind, the philosophy of nominalism put truth and God on shaky ground. God can change and cannot be counted on. In other words, God is arbitrary and his essence is subject to debate.

Universal truths cannot be arbitrary, however. Take for example the question of truth. Truth is truth, whether one believes it or not. There are also universal truths in nature. Water is needed to survive, whether you believe it or not. Gravity holds you to the surface of the earth, whether you believe it or not. The Christian faith holds that God is just and merciful, and he is, whether you believe it or not. This truth of God's justice and mercy can be shaken in the mind of an individual based on an experience with their human father, but the truth is that God remains just and merciful. Based on the philosophy of nominalism, God's character is subject to change because the universal truth of his justice and mercy is denied. In essence, God is arbitrary and one cannot completely put their trust in something that is subject to change. The change that one often imagines is a God who rejects, a God who is vengeful and unfair.

Do you live your daily life with a conscious or unconscious view that God is arbitrary? Do you wonder sometimes if God is going to punish you unjustly? Many of us feel this way because we have had less-than-perfect parents. Maybe you learned that Dad changed after three beers. When he came home after being out at the tavern, you never knew what would happen. Maybe he promised that you would be going to the state fair one day, but instead he flew into a rage about something you did, and he grounded you instead. If this was your experience, you learned that you couldn't trust your father. There was no consistency.

The good news is, though, that Jesus Christ has shown us what the Father is like, and the Church has provided saints for us who are great role models that point to God and what he is like.

Many Catholics live with an unfortunate, warped view of God the Father without realizing it. When something bad happens, they are frozen with fear and confusion, wondering if God is doing something to get even or make them pay. If you had children, would you want them to view you this way? A lack of confidence in God is not a good basis for standing strong in tough times. This way of looking at God will absolutely prevent us from truly praising him because it removes universal truths of God's infinite mercy and love from life's equation. God wants us to know that he is a Father who is faithful, loving, all-knowing, and always there for us. God is not running around looking for opportunities to punish people. Sin carries its own punishment. God wants to rescue you out of your predicament more than you want out of that predicament. God wants to demonstrate his justice, love, and mercy because that is who he is. It is a universal truth whether you believe it or not.

God is the *Father* Almighty, whose fatherhood and power shed light on one another: God reveals his fatherly omnipotence by the way he takes care of our needs; by the filial adoption that he gives us ("I will be a father to you, and you shall be my sons and daughters, says the Lord Almighty"): finally by his infinite mercy, for he displays his power at its height by freely forgiving sins.[2] (CCC 270)

Some people fear that God's power will be unleashed in a manner that appears to contradict what they have learned about him by reading the Bible and through prayer. The *Catechism of the Catholic Church* says, "God's almighty power is in no way arbitrary: 'In God, power, essence, will, intellect, wisdom, and justice are all identical. Nothing therefore can be in God's power which could not be in his just will or his wise intellect'" (CCC 271).[3] When people are unnecessarily afraid of what God might do, it's often because they don't know *him*.

Learning the Language of Praise

Whether you are communicating to a spouse, child, or colleague at work, there is a vocabulary unique to that conversation. The longer you are in a relationship, the broader and more nuanced the vocabulary becomes. My wife and I speak to each other in a language that people usually understand, but there are some pet words and catch phrases that are unique to us that have come out of over thirty-five years of marriage. Over the years we have found many reasons to trust each other and to compliment each other as well.

The art of praising and giving God thanks is a learned discipline springing from the fact that our relationship is, among other things, a bridal-spousal relationship. We are the bride of Christ and Jesus is the bridegroom. Like the communication between a husband and wife, our communication with God, especially in the tough times, should grow deeper and more descriptive with each passing year spent together.

Praise is more than catchphrases, such as "Praise you, Lord! Praise you, Lord—hallelujah! Glory to God! Thank you, Jesus!" Although these words are often incorporated into praise, biblical praise is more robust. It communicates in sentences that describe who God is and what he has done. Praise is descriptive, based on truth, and from the heart. Knowledge of God and the vocabulary to describe it only comes from spending time together. There is a corresponding relationship between time spent in Bible study and prayer and developing a wide-ranging vocabulary suitable to express your heart.

If you do not know the heart of God (theology) or his deeds (economy), there is a very good chance that the vocabulary that you use while trying to praise him will be reduced to catchphrases. A limited vocabulary is appropriate for a child, but more is expected from an adult. I remember back in the early days when I first got excited about God and made a commitment to follow him. My praise vocabulary was limited but heartfelt. As the years went by, my ability to communicate with God grew.

We need to look at what the words we say to God really mean. In essence, they are all commands. *Hallelujah*, for instance, is a command to praise God, so in a sense you are merely barking out a command—*Praise God, Jeff. Praise God, Jeff. Praise God*—but you never get around to actually praising.

You're left with hollow phrases that have no substance, and that substance is what is meant to fill our words. The substance of our praise is who God is. Praise meant to express what we have come to know of him and what he has done in the Bible—his deeds. Instead, most of the time our praise language is reduced to these catch phrases. Praise includes *what*—praise is declaring *who* God is in the midst of our circumstances. It is declaring the facts of who he is.

> Praise is the form of prayer which recognizes most immediately that God is God. It lauds God for his own sake and gives him glory, quite beyond what he does, but simply because HE IS. (CCC 2639)

The content of our prayer should be filled with Scripture, truth, and expressions that renew salvation history in our own lives. Psalm 106:1–2 says:

> Praise the LORD!
> O give thanks to the LORD, for he is good;
>   for his steadfast love endures for ever!
> Who can utter the mighty doings of the LORD,
>   or show forth all his praise?

This is an example of declaring who God is and what he does. Do you see the difference between this and mere catchphrases?

SEEING LIFE FROM GOD'S PERSPECTIVE

When we praise God, we also make a declaration of who we are in light of him. We assess who we are in Christ. That means that when we begin to praise him, we move from our limited power to his unlimited power. We trade our limited wisdom for his unlimited wisdom and our limited experience for his unlimited experience. We move from our perspective to his perspective. In short, we begin to see life through his eyes.

Even when our circumstances are unfavorable, we begin to see them from God's perspective. We trust that God has good plans for us.

> For I know the plans I have for you, says the LORD, plans for welfare and not evil, to give you a future and a hope. (Jeremiah 29:11)

What comes to mind when you hear the phrase "Praise the Lord"? Does it remind you of an excited TV preacher or a psalm response in Mass? Is it an outdated saying only found in the Bible? Whatever this phrase conjures up for you, most of us would agree that giving God praise is important and right—but many of us also don't really know what that means or how to do it.

MORE THAN WORDS

First of all, praising God is more than merely repeating, "Praise the Lord! Praise the Lord!" Too often, our understanding of praise is reduced to catchphrases:

- Praise you, God
- Thank you, Jesus
- Glory to God
- Hallelujah

In other words, we have a limited praise language; there is very little substance to our praise. But biblical praise, as we shall discover later, is more than just words. Biblical praise means that we confess, declare, extol God's greatness, his power, his glory. True biblical praise is a declaration of who God is and what he does (past, present, and future).

This deficiency in our praise language became very real to me many years ago, when I was leading a men's retreat in a remote wooded retreat center in northern Minnesota. During the retreat we were locked in due to a blizzard. We had brought enough supplies to last until the retreat ended on Sunday, but when it came time to leave, the roads were still impassable. There we were, one hundred men, gathered together in the main cabin, with dwindling supplies and no way to get out. To pass the time, since all the men were married, I suggested that we go around the room and share what we were thankful for and what we appreciated about our wives. Now, these were typical Northern Minnesota guys, typically not used to expressing themselves in this way.

After my invitation to talk about our wives there was a long pause. The man on my right stood up in front of the room, saying haltingly, "Well, yeah…okay, well, my wife's name is Peg. Yeah… Peg…quite a gal, Peg." After what seemed like an eternity of stumbling, he began to describe a few things he appreciated about Peg that typified her personality: her love and kindness, things she did with the kids, and so on. He got about a minute into this, and he started crying. Through his tears, he said, "I'm really embarrassed.… I guess I've never really thought about these things. I know one thing's for sure—I've never said them to Peg."

The next guy got up, and he started talking about why he really loved his wife, and he started crying. Before we knew it, we'd gone around the circle, and the whole room was filled with blubbering guys, talking about how much they loved their wives. They'd put *content* to words they'd just normally say superficially—"Yeah, that Peg's quite a gal."

I like to end this story by saying that nine months later, our church grew. (And the women were begging for more men's retreats!)

One of the best ways to illustrate the power of substantive communication is between a husband and wife. Years ago I was in the habit of walking through the door each day after work and casually saying, "Love you, babe" to Emily, my wife. Day after day, those words rolled off my tongue—"Love you, babe" on Monday, "Love you, babe" on Tuesday, and so on. One day, Emily stopped me mid-sentence. "Why?" she asked.

Her request stopped me in my tracks and left me a bit confused as I wasn't quite sure what else she wanted from my statement. I repeated my often-stated greeting: "Because...I love you...babe."

"But tell me *why*," she said. *What more could be said?* I thought. Was she asking me to tell her what I thought of her in detail? Was she asking me to dig up past things she did? Was she asking me to recall various aspects of her personality? What Emily was doing was asking me to put substance to what had become an empty catchphrase. In essence, she was asking me to repeat who I thought she was and what she had done for the previous ten years. *Real* praise involves more than just lip service; it engages the mind *and* the heart. On the receiving end of praise are thoughtful, substantive declarations. By the way, praise will put a smile on the face of your spouse or friend.

THE CONTENT OF PRAISE

Reiterating what I brought up earlier, the substance of praise is connected to both *theology* (the heart of the Father) and *economy* (the works and deeds of God) (CCC 236). Theology refers to God's innermost life within the Trinity (who God is), while economy refers to all the ways God reveals himself and communicates with us (what God does; his works). The more you know who God is, the more you know about his works—and the more you see his works, the deeper you know him and come to rely upon and trust him. Growing in your Christian life means becoming increasingly more familiar with both who God is and what he does. This is what it means to praise God.

And more than just recognizing that God is and that he acts in the world, praise involves knowing who he is in *your* life and what he has done *for you*. This is the content of praise—the *reason* and the *substance*. Without this, praise just remains a hollow exercise.

An episode from my childhood illustrates this. When I was in grade school, one of my favorite pastimes was playing whiffle ball with my friends in the neighborhood. Most of the kids were great, but there were two brothers we tried to steer clear of: the Zimmerman boys. They were the neighborhood bullies, the ones who found great joy in scaring us and threatening us. They were older and bigger than us, so we were scared of them.

One day our ball game expanded in the outfield to the Zimmermans' backyard. The Zimmerman boys saw us and came outside. They put a ladder against the back of their garage, climbed onto the roof, and stood there, watching us and taunting us. I guess I must have been the easiest target, because when they came down, the older of the Zimmermans challenged me to go up on the garage roof like he had. (Little did he know that I actually had a fear of heights because I had fallen off a neighbor's roof a year earlier.) I told him I didn't want to do it. He started to mock me, calling me a chicken in front of all my friends. He could tell I was scared, and he started imitating a chicken, clucking and calling me a baby. Well, finally I gave in and climbed up that ladder. As soon as I got on the roof, the Zimmerman boys proceeded to take the ladder away, leaving me abandoned on top of the roof. All my friends were laughing, and the Zimmermans taunted me even more.

There I was, stranded on the roof—afraid, embarrassed, panicked. So what did I do? Our house was just a few doors down from the Zimmermans, so I went to the edge of that roof and yelled as loud as I could, "Dad! *Dad!*" I didn't yell, "Bob Cavins!" I yelled out according to my relationship with Bob Cavins: "Dad!" The Zimmermans mocked me. "Go ahead, call your daddy." I didn't care—I just yelled louder. And a few minutes later, my dad came flying around the back of that house, and the Zimmerman boys took off. My dad put the ladder back in place, and I came down off that roof and into his arms.

Why did I call my dad? I *knew* that if he heard me, he would come. He had always been there for me in the past. He was faithful. I knew my dad, and I knew his previous actions. Would I have called for him if I had thought he would see me there and say, "You deserve to be there; you are such a dummy. Look at you!"? No. I called on him because I knew he loved me and would help me in spite of my own foolishness.

It's the same way with God. When we know him, we have confidence that, no matter what befalls us, even when it's our own doing, he will be there for us, full of love and mercy.

God is always there for us, and Jesus and the saints are our role models. Sin carries its own punishment—God wants you out of any predicament way more than you do.

THE PURPOSE OF PRAISE

Biblical praise engages both the mind and the heart. We don't chant "Praise the Lord!" like some kind of an incantation that will move God to do something for us. Praise doesn't change God; it should change *us*. It changes our perspective on situations. We move from our limited view to God's unlimited view, and this provides an open door for God to move. So praise also changes our circumstances.

Years ago I went through a health scare that brought about a profound discouragement in my life. In my mid-forties, one of the vertebrae in my neck started to disintegrate leaving me in excruciating pain for months. Similar to the woman with the issue of blood in Mark 5:25–26, who had exhausted all sources to find relief, I visited many doctors, but found no relief from the pain. It seemed that I would be living with this pain for the rest of my life. I could not imagine living like that for forty more years, and I quickly started to sink into darkness, bordering on a sense of hopelessness. It was praising God that turned my attitude around as I recalled who he was and what he had done earlier in my life. In retrospect God had always been faithful and seemed to have a solution to all my problems.

With my eyes fixed on the Lord, he directed me to the people I needed to meet to remedy the situation. I met a priest who told me about a doctor who specialized in neck surgery. It turns out that this surgeon had earlier gone on a cruise with Scott Hahn and me. Although I did not remember the man, I was grateful such a talented man had come into my life. Within weeks I was in the operating room and the doctor had performed what seemed like a miracle. I give credit to God for leading me to the right people and bringing relief to my great predicament. Sometimes God's solutions are different than what we would have imagined. Praise opens the door to a vast array of solutions. Today I am relatively pain-free and thankful for all that God has done.

KEY TAKEAWAYS

- Praising God is more than merely using trite, superficial catch phrases.
- When we understand who God is and what he does, our praise vocabulary grows and deepens.
- We can have complete confidence in God—he is never arbitrary or capricious.
- Biblical praise engages both our mind and our heart.
- Praising God enables us to see life from his perspective.

QUESTIONS FOR REFLECTION

1. Is praising God something you regularly do? If not, why not?
2. What are some ways that you can increase your prayer vocabulary?
3. Do you sometimes see God as being arbitrary? What might cause you to feel this way?
4. How has God acted in your life in the past that you can praise him for?

Chapter Three

THE MANY WORDS AND POSTURES
OF PRAISE

Clap your hands, all you peoples!
Shout to God with loud songs of joy!
— PSALM 47:1

THE BIBLE IS OUR GREATEST RESOURCE FOR LEARNING HOW TO praise God. As you take a look at words and expressions of praise in the Bible, notice how they involve the use of the body. While praise typically takes on a verbal expression, there are times when the body expresses praise to God, and musical instruments can be used as a beautiful expression. Engaging our physical bodies as we express praise to God helps to get our minds focused, just like our rosary beads focus our minds on prayer.

Using our bodies to praise God increases our motivation to praise God. For example, how many times have you forced yourself to get up off your chair and go for a walk only to discover that you thoroughly enjoyed the exercise? You most likely wondered to yourself why you don't walk more often. The same principle applies to praise: At first you may not feel like it, but getting your body to take an active role will change your attitude and perspective.

In the Hebrew language, there are several words to express praise.
Let's look at the ones most commonly used in the Bible.

Yadah

The Hebrew root for the word *praise* is *yadah*, which literally
means to "use the hand"—as in the action of throwing or shooting
an arrow. This definition shows us that praise can be related to a
physical action.

Our bodies were created to praise God, just as our minds and
spirits were. People today are less aware of the importance of
involving their bodies as an act of worship, but in ancient cultures,
the body was a major way of expressing praise to God. Think
about the exuberant dancing and singing of a Gospel choir to get
an idea of how our whole being can praise God. The Bible writers
came from a culture in which people were not afraid to express
themselves through shouts, singing, dancing, musical instruments,
and clapping.

Some of us might want to restrict worship and what we would
describe as "spiritual things" to inward thoughts and meditation,
but worship is meant to employ both body and soul. There's a
principle in Catholic theology that says grace builds on nature.
On the natural level, we communicate with one another and
express our love, our joy, and our passion both in word and deed.
We involve our bodies as part of our expression. This is also true
in our relationship with God. We can certainly meditate and experience inward contemplation, but there is something inside of us
that wants to fully give ourselves to God, which brings in the
physical reality of praise.

Halal

The Hebrew word for praise that we are most familiar with is *halal*, from which we get the word "hallelujah." One meaning for *halal* is "to celebrate or to be clamorously foolish." Exuberant joy over the multitude of good things God gives to us is very fitting. We should be able to express our joy in song, words, shouts, and claps. Do not be ashamed if you run a victory lap around the yard, singing and shouting to God to celebrate his goodness!

I can't help but think of the powerful Hallelujah Chorus from Handel's *Messiah*—the thunderous, joyful sound of many voices that makes everyone rise to their feet and applaud in exultation. *That* is an expression of praise. Through his music, Handel has directed everyone to the majesty and greatness of God.

The Hebrew word *tehillah* is the noun form of the verb *halal* and usually means the "singing of halals." As the psalmist says, "Rejoice in the LORD, O you righteous! / Praise befits the upright" (Psalm 33:1). This verse emphasizes that singing praises to God is what righteous people do. We as the family of God are called to sing praises to God for his great goodness.

Shabach

The term *shabach* means to praise God by a loud announcement, or to laud him as we find in Psalm 145:4—"One generation shall laud thy works to another, / and shall declare thy mighty acts." Declaring the greatness of God to one another is in essence praising God himself. Therefore, when we teach our children and grandchildren about the great acts God has performed both in the Bible and throughout Church history, here too we are bringing our praise to God. Passing on the faith to the next generation is one of the best ways to praise God because it shows God that we care about what he has done for us, so much so that we are eager to pass on the great news to others.

Barak

The Hebrew word *barak* means "to kneel." Kneeling is a natural posture of humility, so putting our bodies into that position brings our minds into a state of quiet where it is easier to remember that God is our Maker. Acknowledging our status before God is a way of exalting or praising God. We are low, and he is high.

As Catholics, we do very well with this physical aspect of praise. We are well acquainted with kneeling before God at various times during the Mass, bowing toward the altar and genuflecting toward the tabernacle. Psalm 95:6 invites us to do this: "O come, let us worship and bow down, / let us kneel before the LORD, our Maker!"

Zamar

The Hebrew word *zamar* means "to praise God with singing or musical instruments." We find this word used in Psalm 21:13. "Be exalted, O LORD, in thy strength! / We will sing and praise thy power."

The use of musical instruments to praise God is definitely encouraged in many of the psalms. "Praise him with timbrel and dance; / praise him with strings and pipe!" (Psalm 150:4).

Todah

An important word, *todah* means "thanks." The term is often used for a particular kind of sacrificial offering. I've devoted an entire chapter to explaining this type of offering in greater detail.

Kavanah

The Hebrew word *kavanah* does not directly translate as praise, but it is an important aspect of praise because it means "purpose, motive, and intention." It can be translated as "attentiveness." We need to have purpose when we approach God to praise him. We should be purposely aware of the wonderful things he has done for us. We don't want to just daydream about God's goodness; we want to engage our minds in a focused manner to direct our praises to God.

Kavanah was necessary when Israel made the ascent to the Temple on the southern steps. Each step up to the sacred mount was shaped in a unique way, forcing the pilgrim to a thoughtful, purposeful ascent to the presence of the Lord. Going into the presence of the Lord required one to direct one's mind and heart to God—to be attentive. This is the essence of *kavanah*.

POSTURES OF PRAISE

There are several ways that Scripture encourages us to praise God, but underlying all of the postures of praise should be an attitude of joy. Psalm 100 always inspires me when I read it; it never fails to put me in a joyful mood.

> Make a joyful noise to the LORD, all the lands!
>> Serve the LORD with gladness!
>> Come into his presence with singing!
>
> Know that the LORD is God!
>> It is he that made us, and we are his;
>> we are his people, and the sheep of his pasture.

Enter his gates with thanksgiving,
and his courts with praise!
Give thanks to him, bless his name!

For the LORD is good;
his steadfast love endures for ever,
and his faithfulness to all generations.

Falling Down

The practice of falling down before a king is something most of us have not encountered. In ancient times, falling down was a sign of homage and surrender to the will of the king. Within the Catholic Church, if you have ever watched the ordination of a priest, you would have seen him lying prostrate on the floor before the bishop to show his willingness to be obedient.

On one occasion, in the middle of the night, I went to the adoration chapel at my parish to pray. As I entered, I was shocked that no one was there, as the consecrated Host in the monstrance should not be left unattended. Our parish has an excellent network of trained volunteers, so I figured something must have gone really wrong for no one to be present. I walked to the center aisle to genuflect, and there was the missing adorer, flat on the floor before the monstrance. I checked to see if the person was breathing, and then, realizing she was okay, I knelt in a pew to begin my prayers. This woman was not sleeping! No, she was praising God in the posture of complete surrender.

"O come, let us worship and bow down,
let us kneel before the LORD, our Maker!" (Psalm 95:6)

Kneeling

As mentioned earlier, kneeling is an act of humility that expresses the proper relationship between a man or woman and God. We are servants of the Lord, and we look to him for everything.

During the years when I was away from the Catholic Church, I really missed the regular practice of kneeling in church. It just seemed like my body was supposed to do that when in the presence of God. For my wife, who was not raised Catholic, kneeling at first was physically difficult, but her RCIA sponsor encouraged her to do it anyway. After nearly twenty years of practice, she finds kneeling for long periods of time not only very easy, but a part of expressing praise that can't be matched by any other form. Kneeling, even without saying a word or praying, is a posture of praise.

Hands Raised

Lifting our hands to heaven can be a form of supplication, but it can also be an expression of praise. In some parishes, the congregation raises their hands at the end of the Lord's Prayer. This is a fitting expression of praise that we see mentioned in the following Psalms.

> So I will bless thee as long as I live;
> I will lift up my hands and call on thy name. (Psalm 63:4)

> Lift up your hands to the holy place,
> and bless the Lord! (Psalm 134:2)

When I was in my late teens, I encountered a group of charismatic Catholics in my home parish. They loved to sing praises to

God with their hands raised, and I felt uplifted by their fervor. I mustered the courage to try it as well and found that I entered a fuller dimension of praise because my body helped me focus more attentively on God as I praised him.

Standing in Awe

Standing is a sign of respect. In times gone by, schoolchildren would stand when a teacher walked into the room. This practice of respect is one that we should bring back! In the first century, disciples would stand as their rabbi sat and taught them. Standing was a sign of respect and a posture of attentiveness. The psalms clearly state that not only should we be in awe of God, we should stand before him.

In Mass, during the Gospel reading, we have the opportunity to express our awe of God by standing in his presence and listening carefully to his words.

> Let all the earth fear the LORD,
>> let all the inhabitants of the world stand in awe of him!
> (Psalm 33:8)

Shouting

A shout to the Lord is an appropriate way to praise God. Our culture knows how to shout at sporting events. If you've ever watched parents on the sidelines during games or even practices on the soccer field where their pint-sized children kick a ball toward a tiny net, they shout encouragement and praise to them without hesitation. We are instructed in Psalm 47:1 to do that same thing. "Clap your hands, all peoples! / Shout to God with loud songs of joy!" Go ahead and give God a shout out now and then for all the amazing things he does. The next time you see a sunset, shout your appreciation of this wonder we often take for granted.

Clapping

I don't know how clapping as a sign of appreciation began, but it seems to be a universal way to communicate praise. Clapping the hands was a common practice in biblical times, both for the praise of men and God. In 2 Kings the people responded to the crowning of a king with clapping.

> Then he brought the king's son out and put the crown on him and *gave him* the testimony; and they made him king and anointed him, and they clapped their hands and said, "*Long* live the king!" (2 Kings 11:12, *NASB*)

Years ago I did the television coverage of Pope John Paul II's visit to the United States for EWTN. When the Holy Father came into the arena in St. Louis, the clapping was deafening. It was a sign from the people that they loved their spiritual father. Their hearts were expressed through their hands.

Playing Musical Instruments

King David appointed musicians to perform before the Ark of the Covenant as a way to praise God continually. In 1 Chronicles 15:16–24, Chenaniah was appointed to be in charge of the musicians because of his skill.

> Praise the LORD with the lyre,
>   make melody to him with the harp of ten strings!
> Sing to him a new song,
>   play skilfully on the strings, with loud shouts. (Psalm 33:2–3)

Singing

Many of us forget that during Mass we are given the opportunity to sing praises to God throughout the liturgy. The chance to sing with one another in the liturgy is something we all can take advantage of doing. It is a common way to convey praise to God. Resist mumbling, turn up the volume, and think about what you are singing. Remember *kavanah* (attentiveness) is important when singing, too.

Dancing

King David himself danced with such abandon before the Ark of the Covenant as it processed into Jerusalem that he embarrassed his wife Michal. Sadly, the repercussion for her bad attitude toward his joy was that she was barren. The point here is that a joyful attitude in the presence of God can be expressed through dancing. Our culture seems to have relegated dancing to nightclubs, and praising God with dancing is looked upon with some skepticism, but dancing before God with the intent of praising him is perfectly acceptable.

Not only do we see how praising God can affect our lives by putting us in a correct relationship with him, it also creates a rightful place for God to dwell. Psalm 22:3 says, "Yet thou art holy, / enthroned on the praises of Israel." Just picture God upon his throne in heaven surrounded by a glorious cloud of praise offered to him from us here on earth and the saints in heaven. Our praise doesn't just float off into nothingness; it gives God his due, for he is holy and completely different than anything else in the universe. This is a wonderful thing to imagine as you praise God.

Key Takeaways

- Praise is so much more than words—we're meant to involve our bodies, too.
- In the Hebrew language, there are multiple words to express the concept of praise.
- We can express praise to God by various postures, and these postures increase our motivation and impact our attitude toward praising God.
- Singing, clapping, shouting, dancing, and playing musical instruments are all part of praising God.

Questions for Reflection

1. If you had to come up with your own definition of praise, what would it be?
2. The next time you spend some quiet time in prayer, choose another posture. If you usually sit quietly, try kneeling or even lying prostrate on the floor. What effect does this have on the quality of your prayer time?
3. At Mass, concentrate on the songs and sung responses; practice singing with *kavanah*. What impact does this have on your worship experience?

Chapter Four

PRAISING GOD IN DIFFICULT SITUATIONS

Let us continually offer up a sacrifice of praise to God,
that is, the fruit of lips that acknowledge his name.

—HEBREWS 13:15

THE STORY OF DAVID AND GOLIATH, FOUND IN 1 SAMUEL 17:1–47, is a great example of biblical praise in action. The very sight of the Philistine giant Goliath instilled fear in the men of Israel. David, however, remembered the times God had saved him in the past and said with total faith, "The LORD who delivered me from the paw of the lion and from the paw of the bear will deliver me from the hand of this Philistine" (1 Samuel 17:37). Clothed in Saul's own armor, David went out to meet Goliath.

When Goliath saw David, he "disdained him; for he was but a youth," and he mocked him and cursed him to his gods. David could have been filled with fear, like the rest of the men of Israel. He could have acknowledged the fact that Goliath was huge, while he was small. He could have suddenly come to his senses, wondering how he had gotten himself into such a predicament. Instead, David stood his ground, and said:

> You come to me with a sword and with a spear and with a javelin; but I come to you in the name of the LORD of hosts, the God of the armies of Israel, whom you have defied. This day the LORD will deliver you into my hand, and I will strike you down, and cut off your head...that all the earth may know that there is a God in Israel, and that all this assembly may know the LORD saves not with sword and spear; for the battle is the LORD's and he will give you into our hand. (1 Samuel 17:45–47)

David looked at the situation from God's perspective, and that completely changed everything. Praising God changed David, and it changed the outcome of a very frightening and challenging situation. Praise changes us; it does not change God.

Another great example of praise in action in a difficult situation is King Jehoshaphat in 2 Chronicles 20. In this story, Jehoshaphat is surrounded by an alliance of three powerful armies. These three armies have converged on the little kingdom of Judah. When the news of the attack reached King Jehoshaphat, his first response was to tremble with fear. This is so typical of our reaction to negative news, isn't it? There might be a report from the doctor. There might be unwelcome news from the human resources department where you work. Maybe you get a call from the principal at your child's high school. Maybe your accountant informs you that you owe a large sum to the government. In those moments, sudden fear just grips you. When what looks like certain defeat is coming your way, often the first reaction is that of overwhelming fear.

After Jehoshaphat's initial reaction, in desperation he turned his attention to God and prayed for deliverance. He saturated his prayer for deliverance with praise. He began by extoling God.

O LORD, God of our fathers, art thou not God in heaven? Dost thou not rule over all the kingdoms of the nations? In thy hand are power and might, so that none is able to withstand thee. (2 Chronicles 20:6)

Jehoshaphat confesses who God is, and this is what praise is. By asking rhetorical questions, he is reminding himself of God's presence and power. He is encouraging himself with what God has done throughout salvation history. We can do the same thing.

Then he adds further praise for past victories that God had wrought and promises he has made (see 2 Chronicles 20:7–9). Jehoshaphat mentions the Temple in particular, reminding God (and himself) that God's presence is there with them. He says, "If evil comes upon us, the sword, judgment, or pestilence, or famine, we will stand before this house, and before thee, for thy name is in this house, and cry to thee in our affliction, and thou wilt hear and save" (2 Chronicles 20:9).

This is a very important point for us. When faced with difficulty, where should you stand? Where the presence of God is. We need to be in God's presence. We can offer up our suffering by going to Mass; we can go to Eucharistic Adoration. Second Chronicles 20:12 goes on to say:

O our God, wilt thou not execute judgment upon them? For we are powerless against this great multitude that is coming against us. We do not know what to do, but our eyes are upon thee.

This is a phenomenal assessment of a challenging situation. How often we, too, find ourselves in situations where we literally don't know what to do. In overwhelming circumstances, we can make up our mind about one thing: our eyes will be on the Lord. When we look to God, we begin to confess who he is and what he has done in our lives. We admit that we are powerless, but our faith is in him. As John said, "For he who is in you is greater than he who is in the world" (1 John 4:4). You may feel powerless—and by all natural means of measuring, you *are* powerless—but if the Lord is with you and your eyes are upon him, it's a whole different ballgame.

Praising God changed Jehoshaphat's fear into faith. He was able to give the people a word from the Lord: "Fear not, and be not dismayed at this great multitude; for the battle is not yours but God's" (2 Chronicles 20:15).

The next day, by faith in God and his promises, Jehoshaphat's army marched onto the battlefield in a very unusual battle formation: They went into battle as a choir. The choir led the attack! When they began to sing and to praise the Lord, the Lord caused the three enemy armies to fight amongst themselves until they annihilated each other (see 2 Chronicles 20:22–23). Not one enemy soldier survived. When God's people decided that the battle was the Lord's, when they looked to him and praised him, God did something about the situation that they could not possibly have done themselves.

We see the same thing in Joshua 4, where Israel is going to enter the Promised Land after four hundred years of Egyptian bondage. The city of Jericho is defeated and taken by praise and thanksgiving; the Israelites were instructed to march around the city, praising God. They did this for six days in a row, and on the seventh day, Joshua gave the triumphant call: "Shout; for the Lord has given you the city" (Joshua 6:16). As they marched around the city for the seventh time, the walls came down and the victory was theirs.

These examples of totally relying on the Lord and praising him are not to say that we have nothing else to do during our battles. Praise goes hand in hand with doing battle. Psalm 149 is a great example of how at times we have to exert our strength and do something about a particular situation. Psalm 149:6–8 says,

> Let the high praises of God be in their throats
>   and two-edged swords in their hands,
> to wreak vengeance on the nations
>   and chastisement on the peoples
> to bind their kings with chains
>   and their nobles with fetters of iron.

Of course, this verse isn't advocating running around violently with swords—the idea is that you do everything that you can do and you rely on God to do everything that God can do.

WHAT GARMENT ARE YOU WEARING?

In Isaiah, God reminds Israel about something he gave them for those times when they might be feeling down.

> The Spirit of the Sovereign LORD is on me,
>   because the LORD has anointed me
>   to proclaim good news to the poor.
> He has sent me to bind up the brokenhearted,
>   to proclaim freedom for the captives
>   and release from darkness for the prisoners,
> to proclaim the year of the LORD's favor
>   and the day of vengeance of our God,

to comfort all who mourn,
   and provide for those who grieve in Zion—
to bestow on them a crown of beauty
   instead of ashes,
the oil of joy
   instead of mourning,
and a garment of praise
   instead of a spirit of despair.
They will be called oaks of righteousness,
   a planting of the LORD
   for the display of his splendor. (Isaiah 61:1–3, *NIV*)

Jesus quotes this same passage in Luke 4:16–21 when he stands up to read in the synagogue. This passage is about proclaiming good tidings to those who are afflicted. When you and I are in tough situations, God does not want us to have a spirit of despair or heaviness. He wants you to wear "a garment of praise instead of a spirit of despair." It is not God's will for you to be in despair or heavyhearted. He wants you to trust him and rely upon him and seek him. He delights in coming to the aid of his sons and daughters, just like a father would. He wants us to show forth his praise. He wants us to show forth his glory. He doesn't want to keep it to himself—he wants to manifest it in our lives.

When I woke up this morning, I stumbled out of bed and into my closet. When I came out I was dressed—all ready to go. This didn't just miraculously happen. I had to put my clothes on. In the same way, God has given you a garment of praise, but you have to put it on! Is it locked away in the closet? Or are you wearing it instead of the spirit of despair? It's an act of your will—it won't happen by accident. No one else is going to do it for you. Begin to praise God and encourage yourself in Scripture. That's putting on the right clothes.

So, the next time you are in the midst of a tough time, don't leave the garment of praise hanging out of sight in your closet. Don't carelessly toss it into a dark corner, where moths can destroy it. No! Put it on, and wear it with confidence. How? By looking to the Lord, just like Jehoshaphat and David did. Initially you might not feel like praising God, but do it anyway. When you feel that spirit of heaviness lift, you'll be glad you did.

PRAISE AS SACRIFICE

Through him then let us continually offer up a sacrifice of praise to God, that is, the fruit of lips that acknowledge his name. Do not neglect to do good and to share what you have, for such sacrifices are pleasing to God. (Hebrews 13:15–16)

What is this sacrifice of praise that God tells us to offer? It's the fruit of our lips; it's confessing who God is and what he has done. Often when the Israelites were faced with a battle, they would offer some sacrifice to God. In fact, King Saul got into trouble because he refused to wait for the priest to come and offer a sacrifice; he offered the sacrifice himself before the big battle. In this situation he took matters into his own hands rather than relying upon God.

We offer our sacrifice of praise to the Lord by our words—but also by our deeds. We acknowledge God, and we do good—we do what is right, even if it looks dangerous. Praising and giving thanks to the Lord involves our whole being.

Many times we find ourselves in a helpless situation, and we cry out to God for his help and intervention. But then, as things start looking like they might work out, we begin to feel that it was just natural, that everything was going to fall into place anyway, and we forget that it was God actually intervening in our life and rescuing us.

There is an old Irish joke about an old man by the name of Mr. O'Malley. As he is driving to the grocery store, he says, "Oh Lord, it has been a long day, and I just need to run in and get a few things. How about if you find me a parking spot? If you find me a good parking spot, I will praise you, and I will go to Mass every day." As he's driving down Main Street, he notices a spot right in front of the store. He says, "Never mind, Lord, I can take care of it from here!"

I think we're all a little bit like Mr. O'Malley. We can go from feeling desperate to immediately forgetting how dependent we are on God's help when we start to see our situation improve. This brings us to the topic of thanksgiving, which we'll be covering in part two of this book. For now, we just want to remember that when God does answer our prayers, whether for something as minor as a parking space or something much more weighty in our lives, we want to bookmark our praise with a thankful heart.

Key Takeaways

- Praising God opens our eyes to seeing him at work in our lives.
- No matter how dire things look, we can make the decision to keep our eyes on God.
- When we praise God with our lips, we also need to do our part by our actions.

- When we praise God and he answers our cries for help, we can't forget to thank him.

QUESTIONS FOR REFLECTION

1. Is there a situation in your life right now that is causing you distress? What has been the fruit of your lips in this situation?

2. Are there any areas of your life where you find yourself wearing the wrong garment? How might you exchange a garment of despair for a garment of praise?

3. What are some of the results in your life when you consciously make a decision to praise God?

Chapter Five

What Happens When We Praise God

Yet thou art holy,
    enthroned on the praises of Israel.
In thee our fathers trusted;
    they trusted, and thou didst deliver them.

—Psalm 22:3–4

W E'VE LOOKED AT HOW GOD ANSWERED PRAYER FOR THE people of the Old Testament—how when they praised him, he acted, often in dramatic ways. In this chapter, we'll look at the impact praise has on situations in our own lives. We'll learn that we can rely on God when we confess both who God is and what he does—his words and deeds.

My wife and I and our three daughters took a trip to Jerusalem. On the last night we were in our hotel room, getting packed and ready to leave for the airport early the next morning. Suddenly my wife, Emily, said in a panic, "Where's Toni's passport?"

"Calm down," I said. "It's got to be here somewhere." The thought did occur to us that my wife might have been pickpocketed because she had put all the passports in her purse when she went into Bethlehem for the day. Our guide—the one who warned everyone else to keep an eye on their stuff—had been pickpocketed on that trip. This doesn't happen all that often, but thieves there are clever.

"Let's just trust God and pray and praise him," I told my girls. I called on St. Anthony: "Help us find it!" We prayed in desperation, "God, you know where it is; we trust you!" We really didn't want to have to go to the hassle of having another passport made.

I went down to the lobby and told our tour guide we lost one of our passports. I went back into the room, and lo and behold, my wife found it in one of the suitcases! Thank you, Jesus!

I could have responded by saying, "I told you so..." Emily could have said, "If only you would have helped me to pack!" That would have only made the situation even more unpleasant and stressful.

In tense situations like this, what is your response? The Bible tells us to be slow to speak, slow to anger (see James 1:19). Stop and calibrate your thinking to God's way of thinking. Tell the Lord, "I don't know what to do, but my eyes are upon you!" Tell those around you, "Let's turn to God." This kind of response allows God an opportunity to enter your life. From there, he can change you *and* your situation. He can do something incredible in your life. Remember, when you begin to praise God, you go from your limited experience, power, insight, and vision to his unlimited perspective, power, insight, and vision, and it gives him the opportunity to do something wonderful in your life.

JUST GET OUT OF THE BOAT

In Matthew 14, the disciples find themselves in a boat in the midst of a raging storm. "The wind was against them." How often do you feel that the wind is against you? Sometimes it feels like *everything* is against you! Jesus never abandons us, though.

During this particular storm, Jesus didn't leave his disciples alone. He came to their aid, but not in the way they expected. Jesus "came to them, walking on the sea" (Matthew 14:25). And what was their reaction? "They were terrified" (Matthew 14:26). They thought they were seeing a ghost! These seasoned fishermen were so terrified that they cried out for fear.

And in the midst of that storm, in the midst of their terror, Jesus immediately spoke to them, saying, "Take heart, it is I; have no fear."

Then Peter got up his courage and boldly said, "Lord, if it is you, bid me come to you on the water" (Matthew 14:28). And Jesus simply said, "Come." No detailed instructions, just a simple, one-word invitation.

And Peter got out of that boat and walked on the water toward Jesus. Suddenly, though, Peter took his eyes off Jesus and began to notice the wind. (Keep in mind, the storm was still going strong.) And when Peter focused on that wind, he was once again afraid. Now full of fear again, he began to sink, calling for Jesus to save him. Jesus grabbed Peter by the hand and said those famous words: "O you of little faith, why did you doubt?" They reached the boat, and the winds died down. The storm was over.

In our own lives, when we are in the midst of circumstances that threaten to overwhelm us, do we recognize Jesus coming to our aid? And when we see him with our eyes of faith, and we hear him bid us to come to him, do we praise him for who he is? Do we get out of the boat?

Just get out of the boat! Being timid and playing it safe are the marks of someone who doesn't know God very well. When you know him you start taking chances. You jump out of the boat, and you walk on water. At times you might sink, but sometimes you figuratively walk on water! That's the great adventure. To get out of the boat is where life changes!

Key Takeaways

- When faced with an upsetting situation, God will always hear and answer our cries for help.
- When we praise God in the midst of some trouble, we build up the faith of those around us as well as our own faith.
- When a storm is raging, choose to recognize Jesus—to see him through the eyes of faith.
- When God calls you, don't hesitate—get out of the boat!

Questions for Reflection

1. Think of a time when you were caught off guard and didn't know which way to turn. What was your response? Did you turn to God, or did you bemoan the situation?
2. Now think of a time when you chose to praise God, even when a situation seemed impossible. What kind of outcome did you experience?
3. Is there a situation in your life today where you are being called by God to get out of the boat? Are you hanging back in fear, playing it safe, or are you living boldly and taking God at his word?

Ten Tips for Praising God

1. Start seeing qualities and deeds in others that are praiseworthy.
Most people recognize greatness when they see it. Young men
know who is great in football or basketball. People in business
recognize the top CEOs and the bestselling authors of motiva-
tional books. Tech-minded individuals know who invented the
Apple computer or founded Microsoft.

One way of cultivating a life of praise is to start spotting in
others those things that stand out and grab your attention. These
are not necessarily big things or things that make the evening news
or the cover of a national magazine, but they are worthy of praise.

At the parish we attend, I started to notice a young mother with
her three little children sitting on the front row during Mass. Her
tender care and attention to her children's needs caught my attention. One Sunday as we drove to church, I told my wife about my
observation and asked if she noticed what I noticed in this young
mother. She had not, but after I pointed it out, she started to see
what I was seeing. After two years of watching this young mother's faithfulness, our paths crossed one day after Mass. I stopped
her and asked to speak with her for a moment. I told her how
impressed I was with her care for her children. I told her that her
kindness inspired me and made me think about my own parenting
skills. She was not aware that people were taking notice, but was
simply acting in a faithful way week in and week out.

Start noticing praiseworthy things in others—and then let them
know. Not only will you be a blessing to them, you also will train
yourself to see the good in others.

2. Begin praising God before difficult meetings at work or home.
I've heard from many businesspeople that the part of their job
they like the least is attending meetings. Occasionally business
meetings contain discussions about difficult decisions and are sure
to be filled with tension. Tension-filled meetings can also happen
at home as parents address issues in the lives of their teens. If the
executive doesn't go into his meeting prepared to resolve conflict
in a charitable way, and if parents don't enter family meetings
with a heart of kindness, explosions can take place.

By taking a few minutes to praise God and look to him, we
calibrate our hearts to the fact that God can do things we are
incapable of. We give him an opportunity to be enthroned in our
situation, and we allow him the opportunity to impart wisdom
and understanding that transcends common wisdom.

By praising God prior to an important engagement, you will
go into the meeting reminded of the heart of God and all that
he has done in the past. In other words, the love of Christ will
constrain your heart, control your tongue, and open your mind
to the impossible.

**3. The next time a difficult situation arises, take a few minutes
before responding to write down two attributes and two deeds of
God that will benefit you in the situation.**
Isn't life fast-paced these days? There doesn't seem to be enough
time in the day to relax and reflect. Instead we tend to move from
one crisis to the next, from one e-mail to the next, constantly
solving problems and putting out fires. The tyranny of the urgent
rules our lives, leaving us empty. In short, we give ourselves to the
urgent things and leave the important things behind. This pattern
leaves us frustrated and void of accomplishing the really important things in our lives.

Often, poor decisions or unkind responses are the result of hasty remarks or imprudent choices. Not taking the necessary time to turn to the Lord often lands us in a more complicated situation than the one in which we began.

The next time you receive that phone call or read an e-mail that spells problems, take a moment to turn to the Lord and write down a couple of his attributes or deeds that remind you of your current situation. Many smartphones have applications that can record notes. If you're not a techie, use note cards to write down your findings. Throughout your trial, turn to your notes and briefly praise God from time to time.

4. Choose a psalm and begin to memorize it. Make it yours. Through memorization the psalm will become deeply embedded in your heart.

In 1982 I joined a friend of mine on a car trip back to my home in Iowa from Florida, where I had been checking out a possible school to attend to further my theological studies. The drive was long, and there were many hours of silence. I started reading the Bible and came upon Galatians 2:20, which says, "I have been crucified with Christ; it is no longer I who live, but Christ who lives in me; and the life I now live in the flesh I live by faith in the Son of God, who loved me and gave himself for me."

On that trip I committed myself to memorizing that verse, and by the time I had returned to Iowa, not only had I memorized it, that verse became my life verse. I have thought of that verse nearly every day since, as it is burned into my heart and mind.

Committing the Word of God, specifically the psalms, to memory is a great way to hide God's Word in your heart. Not only will this have a powerful impact on your current situation, but when you hide his Word in your heart, in a sense you save it for a rainy day. His Word will come back to you in the most opportune times and minister life and hope to you. If you don't put it in, though, it won't be there when you most need it. In addition to God's Word encouraging you, it will also help you in your battle with sin. The psalmist said, "I have laid up thy word in my heart, / that I might not sin against thee" (Psalm 119:11).

Start memorizing a few verses that are particularly meaningful to you, and go over them daily until you know them by heart. It's amazing how many times you will draw on those verses to praise God.

5. Write your own psalm, starting with a petition and ending with praise.
I've often heard people say, "I have a book in me, if I can just get around to writing it." While you might have a book in you, I suspect you also have a psalm in you! What do I mean by this? Real people in real circumstances, experiencing real insights, wrote the psalms.

Those who wrote the praises of God in the psalms were not unlike you. They did not have advanced degrees in psalm-writing, but God moved them to write those things he wanted written for the sake of our salvation. Granted, the psalms are inspired by God—meaning God is the author—but that does not exclude you from writing your own psalm to God.

Years ago I was the pastor of a lively interdenominational church. This was after I grew up Catholic and left the Church, before I returned. I taught a series on the psalms and concluded the series by challenging my friends to write their own psalm. Each person followed the pattern of expressing their heart as it related to their current difficulty. The second half of their psalm was a declaration of who God is and what he has done, and the conclusion was a declaration of victory expressed by mentioning the faithfulness of God.

I asked the members of the church to submit their psalms so the music department could create a song out of one entry. That song would become part of our musical lineup for our times of praise. Once the psalms were submitted, one was chosen and put to music. After we introduced the psalm to the congregation, we asked the author of the psalm to stand. It ended up being an old man who always sat in the back row and never said a thing. Who would have thought that this quiet man could express something so beautiful as the psalm we put to music!

While you may never write anything that is directly inspired by God in the way sacred Scripture is inspired, you can certainly write a psalm that inspires and raises your thoughts and heart to higher ground.

6. Listen to praise music in the car and at home.
There is a powerful story in 1 Samuel 16 that describes how a spirit afflicted King Saul emotionally, leaving him in great need of relief. Music played a key role as young David played his harp, leaving Saul refreshed and free of the troublesome spirit.

> And whenever the evil spirit from God was upon Saul, David took the lyre and played it with his hand; so Saul was refreshed, and was well, and the evil spirit departed from him. (1 Samuel 16:23)

Praise music can be very powerful in moving our hearts. During times of discouragement, when I began to play praise music in the car, my heart was lifted, and I actually was very encouraged and hopeful.

> The musical tradition of the universal Church is a treasure of inestimable value, greater even than that of any other art. The main reason for this pre-eminence is that, as a combination of sacred music and words, it forms a necessary or integral part of solemn liturgy. The composition and singing of inspired psalms, often accompanied by musical instruments, were already closely linked to the liturgical celebrations of the Old Covenant. The Church continues and develops this tradition: "Address...one another in psalms and hymns and spiritual songs, singing and making melody to the Lord with all your heart." "He who sings prays twice." (CCC 1156)

Many people find that they are comforted and inspired when they listen to praise music while driving, exercising, or before going to sleep at night. Praise music has the ability to move your heart, even when mere words seem to fail.

Often I will enter into a praise song by enthusiastically singing along. It is a bit awkward when I'm in full concert mode while driving and pull up to an intersection only to notice the occupant of the car next to me smiling at me in amusement! While the person may think I'm singing a Bob Dylan song, he or she would be surprised to know I'm praising the God of the universe.

7. Create a list of the great attributes of God and post it in your home.

My wife, Emily, and I have three lovely daughters. When they were growing up, we would occasionally deviate from our evening prayer tradition and play a little game. We would go around the room and take turns mentioning two or three things we really appreciated about the other members of the family. Sometimes it was easy, but many times there were long pauses as each child had to dig deep to find something she appreciated about her siblings.

In the same way it is good to occasionally make a list of all the attributes of God that you appreciate. You can include family members in this exercise or just do it privately.

The refrigerator is a great place to post these kinds of lists. You can also make the list into a screen saver that will remind you of God's greatness when you use your computer.

There are many ways to creatively harvest a list of God's attributes. One that I particularly like is using a colored pencil or marker to highlight in your Bible verses that describe God's attributes. Over the months, you will have collected many great descriptions that can act as the core of your list.

You can also use a devotional such as *Magnificat* or *Word Among Us* to help you discover the mighty attributes of God.

8. Participate in a Holy Hour. Adore the Lord in praise and read the psalms.
Once in a while I come home from work or a meeting with a rather bad attitude. The first to discover this attitude in me are my wife and children. There is nothing like a Holy Hour to give you an attitude adjustment! This is a special set aside time to praise God before the Blessed Sacrament. Many Catholic churches have a chapel set aside solely for this purpose.

On those rare occasions when I come home grumpy, my wife will suggest that I head over to the church and spend time with God in prayer. At first I bristle at the suggestion, as it seems to be an admission that I have a problem and she is right. Usually pride gives way to humility, and I take her up on the suggestion and make my way to our parish. Typically I just sit before the Lord with my attitude and he stares back. On those occasions when I open the psalms and begin to enter into the message of a particular psalm, I feel my heart change. By the time I have spent an hour with the Lord, my entire attitude has been converted from being obstinate to being pliable in the hands of God.

A Holy Hour really is the perfect opportunity to exchange your power for his, your wisdom for his wisdom, and your perspective for his. Many parishes provide opportunities to sign up for the same day and time each week, giving you a more structured way of praising God face-to-face.

9. Keep a prayer journal.

Starting a journal is one of those things that initially seems difficult, but if you stick with it, it becomes a habit that yields much fruit.

When I was a young man, I worked for a prominent radio station in Minneapolis, 830 WCCO. My job was to take care of celebrities and well-known sports figures. It wasn't unusual for me to meet rock stars in the morning and actors in the afternoon. While there, I started to keep a journal of my daily encounters. Keeping that journal was a bit of a chore, and I can't say I got a lot out of writing down the day's events just hours after getting home. The payoff came years later when I went back and reread the journals. The emotion, the insights, and the smells of those days came back to me like it was just yesterday. By reading my journals, I was reminded of what I sensed God doing in my life at the time, and I was able to recall his faithfulness at a time when Emily and I were making big life decisions.

The act of remembering is a major theme in the Bible, and it usually points to remembering the great acts of God. When the Israelites crossed the Jordan River and entered the land of Canaan, they left stones in the Jordan as a reminder of what God had done. A journal can be a modern stone for you.

What kind of journal should you keep? There are many options, and the list is as varied as your taste. For those who like to use computers or smartphones there are a plethora of applications to choose from. Many enjoy using a Moleskine paper journal, found at popular bookstores or online.

Keep a journal! You will be blessed when you see the progress you are making, but you will also be encouraged to see the wonderful ways that God has demonstrated his presence in your life.

10. Stay a few minutes after Mass to praise God.

There is no greater action on earth than the action that takes place during Mass. God speaks to us and gives himself as a sacrifice for us. It is in the Mass that the bride (the Church) receives the gift of the bridegroom (Christ). No greater love has been expressed in the world than the gift that was given at Calvary.

To deepen the transference of grace received at Mass, it is a good thing to take just a few minutes when Mass is over to kneel and praise God once again for his greatness. What a beautiful, thoughtful way to walk back out into the world!

PART TWO

Thanksgiving

Chapter   Six

A Biblical Definition of Thanksgiving

> Enter his gates with thanksgiving,
> and his courts with praise!
> Give thanks to him, bless his name!
> —Psalm 100:4

Thanksgiving is more than just a yearly holiday in America where we look forward to celebrating with family and friends. Thanksgiving is meant to be a part of our lives every day. When we are conscious of who God is and what he has done in our lives, we develop a disposition of gratitude. Thanksgiving then becomes the natural expression of that gratitude. Gratitude that stems from thankfulness unites our minds and hearts—it is an expression of our whole being.

Like all expressions of praise, thanksgiving is rooted not only in God's character but also in his actions. Praise and thanksgiving are like two instruments, a duet that communicates the glory of God in an attractive harmony. Praise addresses who God is, the mystery of the Trinity, and thanksgiving recognizes God for what he has done. In the Eucharistic celebration the Church celebrates with "thanksgiving to God the Father for all his benefits" (CCC 1408).

Trying to make a clear distinction between praise and thanksgiving is difficult, because making a distinction between who God is from what he has done is difficult. The two speak to each other and illuminate each other. Notice how both praise and thanksgiving are incorporated into David's expression of gratitude to the Lord in Psalm 30:

> I will extol thee, O LORD, for thou hast drawn me up,
>   and hast not let my foes rejoice over me.
> O LORD my God, I cried to thee for help,
>   and thou hast healed me.
> O LORD, thou hast brought up my soul from Sheol,
>   restored me to life from among those gone down to the
>   Pit.
>
> Sing praises to the LORD, O you his saints,
>   and give thanks to his holy name.
> …
> Thou hast turned for me my mourning into dancing;
>   thou hast loosed my sackcloth
>   and girded me with gladness,
> that my soul may praise thee and not be silent.
> O LORD my God, I will give thanks to thee for ever.
> (1–4, 11–12)

For an example of how praise and thanksgiving are blended, we can look at the sacrament of confession. God acts in a powerful way when he forgives our sins. Our response should be one of great thankfulness. With this in mind, the *Catechism* reminds us that the conclusion of reconciliation is "a prayer of *thanksgiving* and *praise* and dismissal with the blessing of the priest" (CCC

1480, emphasis mine). We praise God for his saving action, and we are thankful for what he has accomplished in our hearts.

THANKSGIVING AND ITS RELATIONSHIP TO BIBLICAL PRAISE

As we begin to delve into this topic of thanksgiving as an expression of gratitude and its relationship to praise, let's take a look at the story of the ten lepers in Luke 17:11–19. It's a short story—only nine verses long—but a very powerful episode.

> On the way to Jerusalem, [Jesus] was passing along between Samaria and Galilee. And as he entered a village, he was met by ten lepers, who stood at a distance and lifted up their voices and said, "Jesus, Master, have mercy on us." When he saw them, he said to them, "Go and show yourselves to the priests." As they went they were cleansed. Then one of them, when he saw he was healed, turned back, praising God with a loud voice; and he fell at Jesus' feet, giving him thanks. Now he was a Samaritan. Then said Jesus, "Were not ten cleansed? Where are the nine? Was no one found to return and give praise to God except this foreigner?" And he said to him, "Rise and go your way; your faith has made you well."

As the story of these lepers illustrates, when we call out to God, asking him for mercy, he comes to our aid. No matter how small our requests (remember Mr. O'Malley and the parking space?), God hears and answers. But just like Mr. O'Malley and nine of the lepers, when we call out to God and he comes through for us, if there is no response, if there is no expression of gratitude, then there is no thankfulness.

We can think of praise and thanksgiving as two bookends. On one side, we have a need, and we ask God for help, making sure to praise him. When we receive an answer to our prayer, we then make sure to express our gratitude with thanksgiving for what he has done. In fact, we often begin to thank God in faith before we even see an answer. We begin not only to praise him, that is confess who he is and what he has done, but we also begin by faith to thank him for his deliverance, mercy, justice, and so on.

A WINNING COMBINATION

Luke 17:15 tells us something quite astonishing. Out of the ten lepers, one of them—when he saw that he was healed—turned around and came back, praising God loudly. He fell on his face at Jesus's feet and gave him thanks. Not only did he call out to God for help, but when he saw that he was healed he continued to praise God, and to that praise he added thanksgiving. Praising *and* thanking God is a winning combination.

Jesus then asked an interesting question. "Were not ten cleansed? Where are the nine?" This is a great question that we need to ask ourselves today. The Church Fathers often teach that the physical healings we see in Scripture are sacramental in a way, pointing to the deep spiritual healing that the love of the Trinity brings with the forgiveness of sins and adoption of sons. The physical healing of blind eyes, for example, is a sign of a deeper healing: the blindness of our hearts. The story of the paralytic is a sign of a deeper healing—we cannot get where we need to go (the beatific vision) without God's help. In the Bible, physical healings are signs of a deeper healing that we are in great need of.

Jesus told this leper, who happened to be a foreigner, "Rise and go your way; your faith has made you well." In a sense all of us are spiritual lepers, but God has made us sons and daughters and, through Christ's sacrifice on the cross, has healed our hearts. How many of us stop regularly and give him thanks? Instead, how much of our life is spent complaining and finding reasons why this or that is not going to work versus praising God and thanking him? A person with a thankful heart has a proper perspective as opposed to those who complain and tend to be self-centered. We all know people who do not express gratitude, and I think we can agree that they are not pleasant to be around. Grateful people, on the other hand, are a joy to be with.

Our praise is a beautiful smell to God. The fruit of our lips and our heartfelt thanksgiving rise up to God as a beautiful aroma, as incense, and everyone around us can sense it too. We become beautiful to be around if we are thankful people. The reverse is true as well: If we are not thankful, we are really hard to be around. We see examples of this all the time, in the workplace, in our families, and in our neighborhoods.

The well-known English preacher Charles H. Spurgeon (1834–1892) once said, "Let your thoughts be psalms, your prayers incense, and your breath praise."[4]

St. Augustine said, "The Christian should be an alleluia from head to foot."[5] This would be a good thing to keep in mind as we begin each new day.

CHECK YOUR HEART

Just as it's important to get regular physicals to check your heart health, it's also important to check your heart where thankfulness is concerned. Where do you stand? What has God done in your life that you can thank him for? If you are having trouble coming up with very much, you might need to ask yourself some hard questions. Are you restless, never satisfied? Are you always thinking about your problems and your circumstances? A lack of gratitude is a clear indicator of a heart turned in on itself, proud and never content.

So take the time to regularly examine your own heart. If you had been one of those ten lepers two thousand years ago, would you have been the one who was grateful—or would you have been one of the nine?

Of course, I know which one you would be. You wouldn't be reading this book if you were not *that* one. You study the Bible; you go to Mass; you pray the rosary. It's a no-brainer—you would have been the one who remembered to say thank you.

Just in case, though, here's a little test to find out if you were the one who was grateful or one of the nine. In the last month, were you filled with praise and thanksgiving, or were you continually complaining about your circumstances? Were you the one that went to Adoration and took the time to thank God? Were you the one that offered praise to God or did you act alone, as if God did not exist? Pope Benedict XVI called this "practical atheism," and he said that this is a greater threat than actual atheism. He explained that actual atheists often think deeply about God before rejecting faith in him, while practical atheism "is even more destructive...because it leads to indifference toward faith and the question of God."[6]

If we're honest, we have all been the thankful one at times and at others one of the other nine. This particular story in Luke provides a great gauge for us to check the condition of our own hearts on any given day or week. We are all spiritual lepers, but God has made us sons and daughters—he has healed our hearts. How many of us stop to give him thanks? How many of us continue to praise and thank him, even in the midst of our difficulties?

In Romans 1:20–32, the apostle Paul examines some of the worst depravities in the world, and he finds that the root of it all is a thankless heart.

> They are without excuse; for although they knew God they did not honor him as God or give thanks to him, but they became futile in their thinking and their senseless minds were darkened. (Romans 1:20–21)

The opposite of this thankless heart is found in the Blessed Virgin Mary in Luke 1:46–49, where she extols the Lord, saying:

> My soul magnifies the Lord,
> and my spirit rejoices in God my Savior,
> for he has regarded the low estate of his handmaiden.
> ...
> He who is mighty has done great things for me,
> and holy is his name.

The Blessed Virgin Mary, Queen of Heaven and our Mother, is a model of praise and thanksgiving. It would be worthwhile to take some time to meditate on the Magnificat and follow her lead. Was she dealing with difficult situations? I guess so! She had just found out that she was pregnant with the Son of God. How was your day?

COOPERATING WITH GOD'S WILL

In the *Catechism*, believing in God is defined as "living in thanksgiving":

It means living in thanksgiving: If God is the only One, everything we are and have comes from him: "What have you that you did not receive?" "What shall I render to the Lord for all his bounty to me?" (CCC 224; emphasis in original)[7]

We often think of God as blessing his children (us), but rarely do we think about blessing God. Blessing God is related to thanksgiving and carries with it the idea of complete adoration and surrender. To bless God is to surrender to his will with thanksgiving. The *Catechism* says:

> Blessing is a divine and life-giving action, the source of which is the Father; his blessing is both word and gift. When applied to man, the word "blessing" means adoration and *surrender to his Creator in thanksgiving.* (CCC 1078, emphasis mine)

The *Catechism* also teaches that obedience to the Ten Commandments is a response to the Lord's loving initiative in salvation history. Obeying the Ten Commandments "is the acknowledgement and homage given to God and a worship of thanksgiving. It is cooperation with the plan God pursues in history" (CCC 2062). In short, we could say that living a life of thanksgiving is living a life that cooperates with God's will.

LIVING IN THANKSGIVING

What does it mean to live in thanksgiving? It involves faith. It means living as though God is the only One—with an awareness that everything we are and everything we have comes from him. Think about it: What do you have that you did not receive? Paul asked the Corinthians this very question in 1 Corinthians 4:7.

And in Psalm 116:12, the psalmist asks, "What shall I render to the LORD / for all his bounty to me?"

The *Catechism* says, "Believing in God, the only One, and loving him with all our being has enormous consequences for our whole life" (CCC 222). And one of those consequences is living in thanksgiving. If you have multiple gods in your life, your allegiance is split and your attitude of gratitude is diluted. But if you truly worship one God, it has great consequences because you then truly live as if God is the only one, and all your thanksgiving is directed to him.

KEY TAKEAWAYS

• While it is difficult to separate praise and thanksgiving, we could say, praise addresses who God is, and thanksgiving recognizes God for what he has done.
• Praise and thanksgiving are like two bookends. On one side, we have a need and we ask God for help, making sure to praise him. When our prayer is answered, we express our gratitude with thanksgiving for what he has done.
• The *Catechism* defines *faith* as "living in thanksgiving."
• Thanking God is a natural response when we live as if God is the only One, not one of many gods.

QUESTIONS FOR REFLECTION

1. Has there been a time in your life where you responded like the nine lepers in Luke that did not offer thanks? Now think of a time when you remembered to thank God for his goodness to you.

2. Take some time to read and reflect on Mary's Magnificat. What can you learn from the way she responded to the events in her life?

3. Do you look at everything—*everything*—in your life as coming from God? Or are there areas where you forget God, where you act like what Benedict XVI called a "practical atheist"?

Chapter Seven

Cultivating a Thankful Heart

Continue steadfastly in prayer,
being watchful in it with thanksgiving.

—Colossians 4:2

Being thankful must become a holy discipline.
Thanksgiving is a choice, an act of the will, especially when you
face unpleasant or distressing situations. You might not *feel*
thankful, but biblical thanksgiving is independent of feelings. You
thank God because it is the right thing to do. Emotions and feelings can (and surprisingly do) follow, but you don't wait until
you feel like thanking God to thank him—because sometimes that
just does not happen. This kind of thanksgiving is a mark of the
mature Christian. A mature believer sees the hand of God in every
circumstance in his or her life. In Ephesians 5:19–20, the apostle
Paul says we are to address one another

> in psalms and hymns and spiritual songs, singing and
> making melody to the Lord with all your heart, always
> and for everything giving thanks in the name of our Lord
> Jesus Christ to God the Father.

Notice that Paul did not say that we should thank God when
things start getting better or when we feel like thanking him. No,

Paul says that we should thank God with our whole hearts—*always and for everything*. In Colossians 3:17, Paul says:

> Whatever you do, in word or deed, do everything in the name of the Lord Jesus, giving thanks to God the Father through him.

Everything really does mean *everything*! There is nothing that we face in life that doesn't involve our attitude toward God: We are called to have a thankful heart no matter what happens. That is why thanksgiving is a matter of the will, not a matter of feelings. This is how love is practiced as well, by the way.

Exercising your will when you don't feel like praising and thanking God is key. Nobody is helpless when it comes to exercising their will and doing what's right. If you struggle with exercising your will, ask God to help you and begin to speak what you know to be true about God.

One mistake people make is equating warm, fuzzy feelings with praise and thanksgiving. The warm feelings may or may not be there, but they have very little to do with the discipline of praising and thanking God. The mature believer, once bad news hits or circumstances suddenly seem dire, if he or she has been cultivating praise and thanksgiving, will turn to God more readily. Just as an athlete who has muscle memory as the result of repeating a move, so mature disciples will turn to God in all circumstances rather than waiting for an emotion to move them. If you navigate through life by emotions, you are certain to be led astray as you will have a fickle guide leading you.

In high school, I was a goalie in hockey. Because I practiced saving shots in glove-saves and kick-outs thousands of times, even today, decades later, while playing with my children in the backyard, when balls are kicked at me in a leisurely game, I have an immediate response to kick them based on those years of goalie practice. I don't even think. It's muscle memory. As believers, we need to develop spiritual muscle memory. I realized this in my own life recently.

Not too long ago, I went to the dermatologist for a routine checkup, and the doctor noticed a mole he didn't like the looks of. Of course he cut it off and sent it to the lab. I wasn't too concerned about it, since I had had other moles removed before, but on the day he called me with the diagnosis, I had a choice of how to react to the news that it was melanoma.

I walked outside into the backyard behind the shed, and I said in response to the news, "Well, Lord, you haven't changed. You are the same yesterday, today, and forever. I have been trusting you all these years, and today with you is just another day. Jesus, I trust you, I trust you, I trust you," and then I just began to praise him for his faithfulness. I recalled how he was faithful in his creation, in my life and in my family's life, and I determined to rest in his faithfulness. I began to thank him for the peace he gave me. I thanked him that he was my physician. Then I returned to the house and told my wife the news, assuring her that God was with us.

Shortly afterward, I underwent surgery to remove the area on my back where the mole had been. As far as the doctor can determine, the cancer has been removed. Naturally my feelings of relief made it easy to thank God for healing, but in the midst of the uncertainty, my attitude of gratitude for whatever may have been the outcome brought peace to our house.

THANK GOD FOR SMALL, EVERYDAY THINGS

Cultivating an attitude of thankfulness means that we don't just thank God for the big things in our lives—we thank him for all the small, ordinary things, too. So often people think they should praise and thank God for the really extraordinary things in their lives, the major battles. But it's an interesting fact: If you don't cultivate the habit of thanking God for everyday, ordinary blessings, you're probably not going to thank him for the major accomplishments in your life, either. Why? Because your heart will have become indifferent to his presence in your life.

Our physical mobility is a good example. If you are already blessed with the use of both your arms and legs, just think how difficult a day seems if one of your limbs is in a cast and you can't use it. It is so easy to take for granted the use of our bodies.

One evening at dinner I was suddenly struck with how amazing our bodies actually are. The family was carrying on the normal dinner conversation, and I reached for the salt shaker and sprinkled a bit onto my food. Suddenly I had an aha moment: My hand did that without me even having to think much about it! I interrupted the conversation to exclaim, "Look! This is amazing! My hand knows how to shake the salt without me even having to think about it! Look!" I kept sprinkling the salt and exclaiming about the wonder of it while the rest of the family looked at me as though I had gone mad. But truly, I was in awe of how remarkable our bodies are and full of thanks that God has created us to do many things with very little effort.

Abraham Joshua Heschel observed that we have lost our ability to walk in awe. He would sometimes begin an evening lecture by announcing that a miracle had just happened. Rabbi

Heschel—with his flowing white hair and beard and his distinctive voice and manner—was a commanding presence, and his audiences were riveted, waiting to find out what the miracle was. Then Heschel told them: "The sun set."[8]

Part of this is due to our inability to see the magnificent and awesome in the small, simple things. Our attention has been distracted by the graphics of digital devices that can eclipse a magnificent sunset or ignore the amazing act of an ant carrying something ten times its weight. If we take time to notice the small, ordinary things of life, our sense of thankfulness can be renewed. The next time you see a sunset, imagine if you had never seen one before. What if no one had ever seen one? People would flock from miles around to see it and even pay for it. Yet every day we are given this miracle from God to enjoy for free! What a gift to give thanks for!

The small things that we so carelessly take for granted are often the things that make our life easier: the ability to eat and digest food, our mobility, our five senses, our incredible brains. Even if you can't walk, there are still amazing things your body and mind can do. The key is to focus on what you do have, not on what you don't have. I was uplifted and motivated recently by several interviews with spectators of the Boston Marathon who lost legs in the tragic bombing. One woman, thirty-two-year-old Adrianne Haslet, a professional ballroom dancer, still saw her life as worth living and made a choice to focus on the positive. She calls herself a fighter and set goals to perform on *Dancing with the Stars* and eventually run in a future Boston Marathon.[9]

Stephen Hawking is thought to be one of the most brilliant theoretical physicists since Einstein. He has more than a dozen honorary degrees and is the former Lucasian Professor at Cambridge, a position held by Isaac Newton back in 1663. Hawking has three children and three grandchildren and keeps an extensive travel and lecture schedule. One of his goals? To make it to space one day.[10]

Obviously, this is a brilliant man who has made incredible contributions to science and physics, someone who lives a very full life. And yet, Stephen Hawking was diagnosed with ALS shortly after he turned twenty-one, and for many years he has been bound to a wheelchair and can communicate only by means of a computerized voice system. His life is an inspiring example of someone who didn't let physical limitations stop him from developing his talents and becoming all he could be.

Think again about those ten lepers in Luke 17. Think of the opportunities for thanksgiving they had during the very next week. Maybe they had never seen their children playing, and now suddenly they get to watch with other family members. Nine of them didn't bother to thank Jesus for their healing. Is it likely that they will even think about thanking him for the small, ordinary joy of watching their children at play?

So develop the habit of thanking God for the seemingly mundane things in life. A sunny day, a good night's sleep, your child's smile, a good cup of coffee, dinner with friends. Once you develop the habit of thanking God, the possibilities are endless. This keeps you full of gratitude, and it also keeps you focused on God and his goodness—as opposed to all the negativity around you.

As Colossians 4:2 says: "Continue steadfastly in prayer, being watchful in it with thanksgiving." A person who has a thankful heart is a person who watches. He or she is on the lookout for the small, ordinary, mundane things in life, realizing that those everyday things become an opportunity to give God glory, to magnify him and give him thanks.

Key Takeaways

- Developing a thankful heart is a spiritual discipline.
- Biblical thanksgiving is independent of feelings and emotions.
- The Bible tells us to be thankful *in all things.*
- Thanking God shouldn't just be reserved for the big events in our lives; we should thank him for small, ordinary things, too.
- Be thankful for what you do have, instead of focusing on what seems to be missing.

QUESTIONS FOR REFLECTION

1. Have you developed the discipline of being thankful, no matter what? Journal about something happening in your life where you don't naturally feel thankful or grateful. How might you change this?
2. What are some small things you can thank God for right now? Write a list of ten things you normally take for granted. As you go through your day, pause to thank God for that small, simple something. Look for blessings in the mundane.
3. Do you know someone who has overcome incredible odds or has serious challenges in life and yet maintains an uplifting, faith-filled attitude of gratitude? What do you think makes this person so positive, while so many others have so much more and are not content?

Chapter Eight

Thanking God in the Midst
of Adversity

Have no anxiety about anything, but in everything
by prayer and supplication with thanksgiving let your
requests be made known to God.

—Philippians 4:6

As we all realize, life can throw us some major curve balls. At times like these, we find that we are quick to turn to God for help. However, in order to make your prayer for help something more than just a begging session, remember to make it a time of thanksgiving as well. God is interested in helping us in times of great need, and he also is interested in filling our everyday needs. The *Catechism* says:

> As in the prayer of petition, every event and need can become an offering of thanksgiving. (CCC 2638)

Every need! This is an important principle. It's not only things we like—a beautiful sunset, for instance—it's the things we *need*, too. Finding yourself suddenly unemployed, a sudden bout of ill health, wayward teens, a conflict at work—the list is endless. There is nothing we can encounter that we can't thank God for.

The letters of St. Paul often begin and end with thanksgiving, and the Lord Jesus is always acknowledged.

Give thanks in all circumstances; for this is the will of God in Christ Jesus for you. (1 Thessalonians 5:18)

And my God will supply every need of yours according to his riches in glory in Christ Jesus. To our God and Father be glory for ever and ever. (Philippians 4:19–20)

But when we encounter things that seem insurmountable, how can we really be thankful? How can we give thanks for stressful times?

Paul gave us the answer in 1 Thessalonians 5:18 when he said, "Give thanks in all circumstances." He modeled this principle of giving God thanks in the midst of adversity when he wrote a letter to the Philippians from his prison cell:

I thank my God in all my remembrance of you, always in every prayer of mine for you all making my prayer with joy, thankful for your partnership in the gospel from the first day until now. And I am sure that he who began a good work in you will bring it to completion at the day of Jesus Christ. (Philippians 1:3–6)

Paul encountered great adversity as he set out to spread the Gospel. He was shipwrecked, beaten, left for dead, persecuted, starving. All in all, he had it pretty rough. If he could thank God in all those things, certainly we can thank God in the situations we face. Even so, Paul wrote those encouraging words while he was imprisoned for the sake of the Gospel. Notice how, in the midst of his situation, he begins by saying that he thanks God in all his remembrances. Obviously he reflected often on the faithfulness of God, and he was especially thankful for the lives of other people. If he was able to thank God, even in the midst of such great adversity, we too can learn to be thankful.

God is always more powerful than any situation we find ourselves in, so we must learn to entrust ourselves to him like Paul did. We must thank God in all things. During a difficult time in our teen-raising years, my wife and a dear friend challenged each other to pray a fifty-four-day novena for a particular situation. Novenas usually involve both a petition and thanksgiving over a nine-day period; however, my wife and her friend decided a novena times six was in order for this situation. I prayed the rosary with Emily on the days I could, and for the first half of this long novena, we had no problem asking God for help.

However, after twenty-seven days when the novena switched to giving thanks each day for the situation, we realized how hard it was to be thankful. We would look at each other and ponder for a while what we could possibly be thankful for during the next twenty-seven days. Thanks be to God, though, we stuck it out and continued to give thanks. Each day we found that, although the situation seemed to be the same, our hearts were changing so God could receive glory even in the midst of it all.

St. John Chrysostom understood what St. Paul meant. He wrote:

Give we thanks then in all things; whatever may have happened; for this is thankfulness. For to do so in prosperity indeed, is no great thing, for the nature of the circumstances of itself impels one thereto; but when being in extremities we give thanks, then it is admirable. For when, in circumstances under which others blaspheme, and exclaim discontentedly, we give thanks, see how great a philosophy is here. First, thou hast rejoiced in God; next, thou hast shamed the devil; thirdly, thou hast even made that which hath happened to be nothing; for all at once, thou both givest thanks, and God cuts short the pain, and the devil departs.[11]

There are many examples in the Bible of acknowledging God in times of adversity. When Paul and Silas were in prison. They could have wallowed in discouragement, feeling abandoned, but instead they chose to sing praises to God.

But about midnight Paul and Silas were praying and singing hymns to God, and the prisoners were listening to them, and suddenly there was a great earthquake, so that the foundations of the prison were shaken; and immediately all the doors were opened and every one's fetters were unfastened. When the jailer woke and saw that the prison doors were open, he drew his sword and was about to kill himself, supposing that the prisoners had escaped. But Paul cried with a loud voice, "Do not harm yourself, for we are all here." (Acts 16:25–28)

Even more inspiring is the story of Stephen in Acts 7:54–60. Even as he was being stoned to death, he glorified God through his torture.

Now when they heard these things they were enraged, and they ground their teeth against him. But he, full of the Holy Spirit, gazed into heaven and saw the glory of God, and Jesus standing at the right hand of God; and he said, "Behold, I see the heavens opened, and the Son of man standing at the right hand of God." But they cried out with a loud voice and stopped their ears and rushed together upon him. Then they cast him out of the city and stoned him; and the witnesses laid down their garments at the feet of a young man named Saul. And as they were stoning Stephen, he prayed, "Lord Jesus, receive my spirit." And he knelt down and cried with a loud voice, "Lord, do not hold this sin against them." And when he had said this, he fell asleep.

As these examples show, thanking and praising God is not reserved for the calm before or after the storm! Amazing things happen when we praise and thank God in the very midst of our trials.

Start now to thank God for the good things so that when adversity comes, you are in the habit of praising and thanking him in the hard times. If the habit of praise and thanksgiving is not cultivated prior to being in the midst of a difficulty, the odds of you praising God and thanking him during that difficult time are very slim. Ironically, it's the good times and the daily discipline of praise when things seem to be going fine that will determine how you act when things are not so fine.

How we respond in the midst of difficulty also gives us an opportunity to teach our children how to respond to good times and bad and provides them with an opportunity to glorify God. The odds of your children responding to challenges the way you do is pretty good, so remember that your challenge also means that your children's classroom of life is open.

On one occasion, I was in my home office on the phone, and my youngest daughter came in unannounced. She was probably about four years old at the time. At first I wanted to shoo her out because I was on an important call, but then I saw that she was holding a bottle of holy water. She wanted to bless me with it! She had seen us bless things with holy water, and she wanted to do it, too. Children want to imitate us, so if they observe us thanking God when hard times come, they will be motivated and equipped to thank God themselves when the time comes.

We could say that your trouble becomes a big stage on which you can glorify God. There are people watching—you have an audience!

KEY TAKEAWAYS

- There is no need that God is not interested in filling in our lives; we are to bring every need to him.
- The Bible is full of examples of those who gave thanks in the midst of great adversity.
- The time to develop the habit of being thankful is *before* adversity strikes.
- Responding with praise and thanksgiving in the midst of adversity provides a powerful lesson for our children.

QUESTIONS FOR REFLECTION

1. Are there needs in your life that you hesitate to bring before the Lord? If so, why?
2. As you look back on the past year, what adversity have you faced, and how did you handle it?
3. If those around you tend to respond negatively to challenges and difficulties, how are you able to remain positive and exhibit thankfulness?

Chapter Nine

Saying Thank You:
The *Todah* Offering

I will offer to thee the sacrifice of thanksgiving
and call on the name of the Lord.

—Psalm 116:17

Howa many times have you gotten yourself into a sticky
situation and promised God that if you got out of it you would
change some bad habit or do some good deed? In the 1978 film
The End the main character Sonny (Burt Reynolds) learns he only
has six months to live. His way of coping with this unwelcome
news is to attempt suicide by swimming out into the ocean in
the hope of drowning. After swimming quite a distance into the
ocean, Sonny exclaims, "Here I come, Lord!" and then plunges
down into the deep water. After a period of silence, accompanied by the soundtrack of his son questioning where he went, the
viewer is left to wonder if he is in fact dead. Suddenly Sonny rises
out of the water, gasping for breath and yelling, "I want to live!"
After realizing how far out into the ocean he is, he starts to swim
toward shore, saying, "I can never make it."

As he continues to swim, he says, "If you save me, God, I'll give you everything—100 percent—I'll give you everything that I own. Dear God, please save me! I don't want to die." He keeps swimming toward the shore, unsure whether he can make it.

He looks up, sees the trees in the distance, and says, "Please God, save me! I don't know if I'm going to make it. Save me! If I make it, 50 percent of everything I've got is yours."

He keeps swimming. He then sees the trees cresting on the horizon and exclaims, "Please God, help me make the last twenty yards! If you save me, 10 percent of everything I've got is yours."

When Sonny finally makes it to shore, he turns over, spits out the water, looks up at the sky, and says, "You know, God, you got some nerve, asking for everything I've got."[12]

How many times do we cry out to God in distress and promise the world to him, only to go back on our word when all is clear? Everyone who finds himself in a dilemma intuitively turns to God and makes promises, whether they are empty or sincere. Our natural tendency is to promise God 100 percent, but when we discover we are fine, we ignore our promise and may even say it was God's fault in the first place. But, as we can learn from Scripture and the sacrificial system of the Israelites, there is a prescribed way to give God thanks for all that he has done for us, especially when he helps us through a perilous time.

THE *TODAH* OFFERING

In the Old Testament, there were several kinds of sacrifices, such as burnt offerings and grain offerings, which were performed for specific reasons. The one with which we are most familiar is the Passover sacrifice, but there was another offering—called the *todah* offering—that was very significant. The Hebrew word *todah* means "thanksgiving," and this word is used in modern Hebrew today to say "thank you."

From a biblical perspective, thanksgiving is more than just a personal expression from an individual filled with gratitude. Thanksgiving characterizes the people of God and is raised to a liturgical level as an expression of trust in God who saves. In the Old Testament, this liturgical form was the *todah* offering, whereas within the Catholic Church, this offering is the Eucharist.

The book of Leviticus describes the *todah* sacrifice in more detail. Notice how the offering is accompanied by unleavened bread, revealing the connection between the *todah* offering and the Eucharist.

> And this is the law of the sacrifice of peace offerings which one may offer to the LORD. If he offers it for a thanksgiving, then he shall offer with the thank offering unleavened cakes mixed with oil, unleavened wafers spread with oil, and cakes of fine flour well mixed with oil. With the sacrifice of his peace offerings for thanksgiving he shall bring his offering with cakes of leavened bread. And of such he shall offer one cake from each offering, as an offering to the LORD; it shall belong to the priest who throws the blood of the peace offerings. And the flesh of the sacrifice of his peace offerings for thanksgiving shall be eaten on the day of his offering; he shall not leave any of it until the morning. (Leviticus 7:11–15)

The *todah* is a subcategory of the peace offering mentioned in Leviticus. As we will see by the example of Jonah, the *todah* sacrifice was a thank offering from someone whose life had been saved from great danger, such as war or a natural disaster. Sonny should have made this kind of offering after he was saved from the ocean!

Jonah, who found himself in what looked like a fatal situation in the belly of the whale, committed to a *todah* offering in the Temple if he survived. Jonah promised God that he would pay his vow if he saved him.

> But I with the voice of thanksgiving
>   will sacrifice to thee;
> what I have vowed I will pay.
>   Deliverance belongs to the LORD! (Jonah 2:9)

Jonah realizes that God is his source for salvation, and he has every intention to acknowledge that once he makes it back to the Jerusalem Temple alive.

DETAILS OF THE *TODAH* OFFERING

What would a typical *todah* offering look like? First, a person would bring an animal, in Jonah's case a lamb, to the Temple and present it to the priest, who would sacrifice it on the altar and then roast it. The Law of Moses commanded that the sacrifice be eaten on the same day as the offering was made, and so family and friends were invited to a meal in order that all of it was consumed. Along with the lamb, unleavened bread was presented to the Lord and eaten at the meal along with wine. Psalms of thanksgiving accompanied the meal in order to commemorate the occasion and show gratitude. Many psalms are considered to be psalms of thanksgiving, such as Psalms 22, 69, and 116.

If you are familiar with the Passover meal, you'll recognize that it seems to be a type of *todah* offering, because the elements of the lamb, bread, and wine are present along with singing psalms in praise to God for his mighty deliverance from Egypt. Many scholars today also see the connection between the Passover sacrifice and the *todah* offering at the Lord's Last Supper meal. The focus of one's heart and mind during the *todah* meal is to recall the saving actions of the Lord. Thanksgiving and remembrance go hand in hand in the life of a believer.

During the reign of King David, the *todah* offering was raised to a liturgical level when he appointed a priest to guard the Ark of the Covenant while it was housed in the city of Obed-Edom (before it was brought to Jerusalem). David's victory over the Canaanites completed the conquest of Canaan and made way for the permanent Temple to be built in Jerusalem. This great occasion was marked by a *todah* offering and was shared with all the people of Israel:

> And they brought the ark of God, and set it inside the tent which David had pitched for it; and they offered burnt offerings and peace offerings before God. And when David had finished offering the burnt offerings and the peace offerings, he blessed the people in the name of the LORD, and distributed to all Israel, both men and women, to each a loaf of bread, a portion of meat, and a cake of raisins. (1 Chronicles 16:1–3)

Next, King David appointed Levites to praise the Lord before the Ark of the Covenant. Thanksgiving was so central to the Israelite's liturgical worship that King David also appointed Asaph and his brethren to continually offer thanks and praise to God.

> Moreover he appointed certain of the Levites as ministers before the ark of the LORD, to invoke, to thank, and to

praise the LORD, the God of Israel. Asaph was the chief, and second to him were Zechariah, Je-iel, Shemiramoth, Jehiel, Mattithiah, Eliab, Benaiah, Obed-edom, and Je-iel, who were to play harps and lyres; Asaph was to sound the cymbals, and Benaiah and Jahaziel the priests were to blow trumpets continually, before the ark of the covenant of God. (1 Chronicles 16:4–6)

1 Chronicles 16:7–36 contains the psalm that Asaph was to sing commemorating God's mighty deeds. Here is a portion of the psalm:

> Then on that day David first appointed that thanksgiving
> be sung to the LORD by Asaph and his brethren.
> "O give thanks to the LORD, call on his name,
>   make known his deeds among the peoples!
> Sing to him, sing praises to him,
>   tell of all his wonderful works!
> Glory in his holy name;
>   let the hearts of those who seek the LORD rejoice!
> Seek the LORD and his strength,
>   seek his presence continually!
> Remember the wonderful works that he has done,
>   the wonders he wrought, the judgments he uttered,
> O offspring of Abraham his servant,
>   sons of Jacob, his chosen ones!" (1 Chronicles 16:7–13)

This became a continual offering in the Temple, known as a liturgy of thanksgiving, which used the psalter as the songbook for the sacrifice. King David divided the Levites into twenty-four groups. Two groups served each month, one during the night and one during the day, so that praise and thanksgiving was offered around the clock. Not only is perpetual adoration of God at the heart of the Temple liturgy, we see it echoed in Revelation in the heavenly Temple. In Revelation 24, elders praised God in the heavenly throne room: clearly a reflection of the twenty-four Levites in the Temple.

We can see from this that perpetual adoration is not something the Catholic Church made up. It's part of the fabric of what it means to be God's people: We are created for the praise of his glory, and our praises join with those of the saints in heaven.

FROM PLIGHT TO PRAISE

Using psalms is a crucial part of expressing thanks to God. King Hezekiah offered a *todah* song to God after recovering from a serious illness. A closer look at Isaiah 38 demonstrates the structure of the *todah* song and offers practical tips on how to make thanksgiving personal in our own lives.

The pattern seen in Hezekiah could be described as going from *plight* to *praise*. Dr. Tim Gray describes well this movement:

> For instance, someone finds himself in a life-threatening situation, encountering serious sufferings. Then he calls out to the Lord with a lament, recounting his bitter experience to God (verses 10–15). This lament is accompanied with hope and faith, as the sufferer calls out to God for deliverance (verses 16–18). The Lord answers with deliverance, and the lament turns into praise and thanksgiving (verses 19–20). The one who has been redeemed gathers friends and family (notice the "we" of Hezekiah's psalm, describing the corporate aspect of those who go to the temple to sing God's praises) to give thanks to God with

a public demonstration of praise, which is marked with testimony of God's faithfulness and loving kindness. This is the pattern of *todah*, the pattern of Israel's praise.[13]

With the *todah* offering as the backdrop, the Last Supper comes into clear focus. The Greek word for the Hebrew *todah* is *eucharistia*, which means "thanksgiving." From early on, Christians referred to the Lord's Supper as the *Eucharist*. Justin Martyr, back in A.D. 155 described the Eucharist and how the word was used in prayer by repeatedly referring to the Greek term *eucharistia*.[14]

Taken from Jesus's own words in Luke 22:19, Jesus took the bread and wine and gave "thanks" (*eucharistia*). Thanksgiving is what defines the Mass, and every believer attending Mass should be aware of this fact. But how many of us really are? The *Catechism* says:

> The Eucharist is a sacrifice of thanksgiving to the Father, a blessing by which the Church expresses her gratitude to God for all his benefits, for all that he has accomplished through creation, redemption, and sanctification. Eucharist means first of all "thanksgiving." (CCC 1360)

Dr. Gray points out that the Eucharist is both a Passover and *todah* offering in one, as the Passover meal has the form and content of a *todah* offering.[15]

Often we come to Mass fully feeling the impact of our lives' dilemmas. It is here, in the Mass, that we bring our plight to God and recall his saving actions. Jesus, as the new David and the great high priest, leads us in thanks to the Father for the salvation he has brought us. We offer up thanksgiving to God in the Mass and celebrate the victory of our risen Lord. The victory of Christ in the Mass is our victory as we are joined with him through his body. Every time we enter into the Mass with a sense of plight, we should exit with praise and thanksgiving in our hearts and on our lips.

The Mass is the great *todah* offering that celebrates the New Exodus from sin and bondage. As the Passover was Israel's national *todah* meal, the Eucharist is the Church's *todah* meal. Jesus said, "Do this in remembrance of me" (Luke 22:19). We are called to remember, with grateful and thankful hearts, what Christ did for us on the cross. Truly it is the cross that holds the key to our moving from plight to praise!

If we fully enter into the Mass with our minds and hearts and recall the saving actions of God, it should result in a deeper trust in the One who loved us and died for us. Remembering Jesus by celebrating this memorial of his death and resurrection should create in us a *philio* trust—a deep, family bond of security.

It is interesting to note that the ancient Jewish rabbis made a significant prophecy that is recorded in the Hebrew *Midrash*. The ancient prophecy states:

> In the coming Messianic age all sacrifices will cease, but the thank offering [todah] will never cease.[16]

After the destruction of the Temple in A.D. 70, the animal sacrifices indeed did cease, but thanks be to God, the *todah* offering continued on with the Eucharist. Each week, the Lord's Supper was commemorated, and the flesh of Christ in the form of bread was consumed by those who followed Christ's teachings.

THE CENTER OF IT ALL

Since the Eucharistic celebration is the center of the Christian faith, and all other sacraments orbit the real presence of Christ, to be a Catholic Christian means that thanksgiving is at the center of our lives. We learn through the liturgy that we are called to be a people of thanksgiving, and we realize that an attitude of thankfulness continues on in our lives even when the Mass is ended.

The sheer number of times that thanksgiving is mentioned in the Mass should alert us to just how important thanksgiving is in our lives. There is an axiom that we follow as Catholics: *Lex Orandi, Lex Credendi, Lex Vivendi.* This means: "As we worship, so we believe, so we live." We realize that thanksgiving is at the center of our worship, and so we believe. Believing that thanksgiving is central to our lives results in living our lives in such a way that every thought and action is influenced by thankfulness. If we are not truly present during Mass, physically and mentally, engaging our intellect and will, the odds of worship translating into life transforming action will diminish. In other words, the victory you so desire to overcome life's challenges has a lot to do with how you worship.

This concept of the Mass being the epicenter for overcoming battles was not foreign to the early apostles. St. John understood the relationship between the liturgy in heaven and the battles on earth. Speaking of the defeat of the devil in the book of Revelation, he said, "And they have conquered him by the blood of the Lamb and by the word of their testimony, for they loved not their lives even unto death" (Revelation 12:11).

The sad fact, though—and one that needs to be addressed in all of our lives—is that often there is a gap between our faith and our everyday life. In other words, we say we believe, but our everyday activity does not reflect it. It's a lifestyle of a practical atheist—believing in God but living as if he didn't exist. Pope Paul

VI taught that this split was one of the most serious errors of his day, and it's even more true today. The Vatican II document *Gaudium et Spes* says:

This council exhorts Christians, as citizens of two cities, to strive to discharge their earthly duties conscientiously and in response to the Gospel spirit. They are mistaken who, knowing that we have here no abiding city but seek one which is to come, think that they may therefore shirk their earthly responsibilities. For they are forgetting that by the faith itself they are more obliged than ever to measure up to these duties, each according to his proper vocation. Nor, on the contrary, are they any less wide of the mark who think that religion consists in acts of worship alone and in the discharge of certain moral obligations, and who imagine they can plunge themselves into earthly affairs in such a way as to imply that these are altogether divorced from the religious life. This split between the faith which many profess and their daily lives deserves to be counted among the more serious errors of our age. Long since, the Prophets of the Old Testament fought vehemently against this scandal and even more so did Jesus Christ himself in the New Testament threaten it with grave punishments. Therefore, let there be no false opposition between professional and social activities on the one part, and religious life on the other. The Christian who neglects his temporal duties, neglects his duties toward his neighbor and even God, and jeopardizes his eternal salvation. Christians should rather rejoice that, following the example of Christ Who worked as an artisan, they are free to give proper exercise to all their earthly activities and to their humane, domestic, professional, social and technical enterprises by gathering them into one vital synthesis with religious values, under whose supreme direction all things are harmonized unto God's glory. (43)

Giving God thanks in everyday activities bridges this gap and integrates our lives in such a way that we become whole, healed, and filled with joy.

KEY TAKEAWAYS

- When God rescues us from a disastrous situation, we can thank him just like the Israelites did.
- The *todah* is still the way modern Israelites say thank you.
- The way we worship dictates the way we believe, and this impacts the way we live.
- Thanksgiving bridges the gap between our lives and our faith.

QUESTIONS FOR REFLECTION

1. Have you ever been in a sticky situation like Burt Reynolds's character in *The End*? Did you find yourself going back on certain promises once the crisis had passed?
2. How can you deepen your experience of being at Mass so it can more authentically transform your life?
3. Is there a gap between what you say you believe and how this plays out in real life? Do you see any evidence of acting like a practical atheist in your life?

Chapter Ten

DAILY EXPRESS YOUR THANKS TO GOD

And they shall stand every morning, thanking and
praising the LORD, and likewise at evening.

— 1 CHRONICLES 23:30

WE TAKE TIME EVERY DAY TO BRUSH OUR TEETH AND SHOWER,
but have we made it a habit to start our day with thanks to God?
In ancient Israel, a daily habit of thanksgiving was so important
to the life of the nation that the Levites were officially appointed
to stand in the Temple every morning and evening to do one thing:
thank God. Thanksgiving was so important to the Israelites that
they actually appointed people to represent them by thanking
God every morning and every night, as the above verse says.

We have a modern-day corollary: Eucharistic Adoration. During
Adoration, we ask people to sign up to be with God, spending
time in front of the exposed monstrance, praying, praising,
and thanking God in Christ. Adoration is a marvelous thing!
Paragraph 1418 in the *Catechism* tells us:

> Because Christ himself is present in the sacrament of the
> altar, he is to be honored with the worship of adoration.
> "To visit the Blessed Sacrament is...a proof of gratitude,
> an expression of love, and a duty of adoration toward
> Christ our Lord."[17]

When we go to Adoration, we are following the pattern begun in the Old Testament—to be in the presence of the Lord and take time to speak to him with thanksgiving. This is the proof of a heart filled with gratitude.

Daniel knelt three times a day to give thanks to God. Daniel 6:10 tells us that Daniel went to his house, where his open windows faced Jerusalem, and "he got down upon his knees three times a day and prayed and gave thanks before his God." Three times every single day, Daniel would get down on his knees and thank God. What is our excuse?

The Church has afforded us with many ways to participate in thanking God each day. Just as the Jews prayed three times a day, within the Catholic tradition there is the discipline of praise known as the Liturgy of the Hours. This is a compilation of prayers, psalms, Scriptures, and readings that is read corporately among clergy and religious throughout the day, from morning until night. All Catholics can pray these daily prayers and thank God with the entire Church by praying along with the Liturgy of the Hours. You can find these in book form at a local Catholic bookstore, and now there are handy apps for your smart phone that provide the daily readings.

As Daria Sockey writes in *The Everyday Catholic's Guide to the Liturgy of the Hours*:

> Although it is possible to pray in our own words, or with favorite devotions, there is something powerful and satisfying about using the same words and forms used by millions of believers on each particular morning, midday, and evening. Praying the Liturgy of the Hours brings home the meaning of that phrase in the Creed, "I believe

in the communion of saints." We, the faithful on earth, the saints in training, are joined in a unique way as we pray the psalms and canticles appointed to each day.[18]

In the Christian tradition, time is sanctified. In reality, all time is Christ's time. As the first affirmation of the Easter Vigil says: "All time belongs to Christ, and all the ages! To him be glory and power for all the ages!"[19] And there's no better way to fill that time than by praise and thanksgiving; it's a fitting response to acknowledging Christ's ownership of time. As Christians, we don't understand the passing of time—days, months, seasons, years—the way the world does; instead, we see them from the perspective of the Resurrection. We see God's glory reflected in every moment.

In addition to Adoration, there are many other practical things you can do. Many of us have good intentions, but it's easy to get caught up in the day's busyness. In order to cement the practice of being thankful throughout the day, look for ways to make it fun and creative. What could you do that would help you remember to give thanks to God throughout the day?

You can set the alarm on your wristwatch to go off at noon so you can stop and pray the Angelus, or at three o'clock in the afternoon for the Chaplet of Divine Mercy. What if you set your alarm every day at a certain time just to thank the Lord, like Daniel did? You can send yourself an e-mail or text message as a reminder.

There are lots of opportunities for acknowledging God throughout the day. Turn off the radio in the car. Take a break from listening to that podcast once in a while. Turn the television off and thank God in the silence. Pray a rosary instead of filling yourself with needless data. There are all kinds of simple and practical ways for you to regularly praise and thank God.

One way my wife puts thanksgiving into practice is by using traffic lights as she drives. By her own admission, she can become very impatient waiting at red lights, so in order to avoid becoming frustrated waiting for the light to turn green, she decided to thank God for all the blessings she could think of before the light changed. In this way, she actually looks forward to a red light so she can express her appreciation to God rather than stewing about the wait. We live in an area with many traffic signals, so this practice is used many times on a daily basis.

THANKSGIVING IN THE EXAMEN

The Mass is the supreme prayer of the Church, but there are other types of prayers that incorporate thanksgiving as well. One of the great Ignatian spiritual exercises is the Examen, a beautiful prayer encounter with Christ resulting in a transformed life. Below I have outlined the five steps in the Examen, but it is the first step that I would like to focus on in this rich exercise.

1. *Gratitude.* You take notice of the wonderful gifts that God has placed in your life and take a few moments to acknowledge God's gifts by exercising thanksgiving. In this step you walk in gratitude.

2. *Petition.* Ask God for a particular insight.

3. *Review.* With God, review the day and look for those things that move your heart. Pay attention to particular thoughts and stirrings of the heart. Take note of those things that are not of God. Examine the choices you've made.

4. *Forgiveness.* Ask God for forgiveness, and ask him to remove the burdens of your heart.

5. *Renewal.* Begin to look to the next day and determine in your heart how you are going to live tomorrow according to his will. Leave with an optimistic expectation.

There are many ways to conduct a spiritual exercise that examines your heart. You could begin by assessing your growth, thinking about an attribute of God, or asking others what they notice about you, but for St. Ignatius gratitude was the first step in his Examen—"to give thanks to God our Lord for the benefits received."[20]

Why would St. Ignatius start with thanking God? From the moment of his conversion, St. Ignatius was keenly aware that God poured out gifts in abundance. The fact that God gives and gives provided St. Ignatius with a profound sense of being loved by God and also the realization that God could use him. Fr. Timothy M. Gallagher, in his book entitled *The Examen Prayer: Ignatian Wisdom for Our Lives Today*, wrote:

> When Ignatius tells us that the examen begins with gratitude for God's concrete gifts during the day, he is opening a window into the deepest reality of our spiritual lives: God's unbounded love for us and desire for our response, in love, to the love revealed in this giving.[21]

St. Ignatius explained how important gratitude is. He wrote:

> May the highest grace and the everlasting love of Christ our Lord be our never-failing protection and help. It seems to me, in the light of the divine Goodness, though

others may think differently, that ingratitude is one of the things most worthy of detestation before our Creator and Lord, and before all creatures capable of his divine and everlasting glory, out of all the evils and sins which can be imagined. For it is a failure to recognize the good things, the graces, and the gifts received. As such, it is the cause, beginning, and origin of all evils and sins. On the contrary, recognition and gratitude for the good things and gifts received is greatly loved and esteemed both in heaven and on earth.[22]

St. Ignatius became aware of God's good gifts on a daily basis, by purposefully recounting what God had given him. God's gifts were a sign that God did indeed love Ignatius and was involved in his life. This purposeful exercise of taking inventory of God's abundant gifts acted as a trigger that released an attitude of gratefulness expressed by thanksgiving.

For St. Ignatius, this first step in the Examen of "giving thanks to God our Lord for the benefits received" resulted in a deep understanding that he was personally loved. As we covered in the section on praise, trust is the factor that will determine whether we turn to God and accept who he is and what he has done. By recounting God's gifts, St. Ignatius did not have to manufacture thanks or force himself to be thankful; thanksgiving was the result of the simple observation of what God had done in his life. In other words, St. Ignatius responded to what God did first.

Realizing that all thankfulness is a response to what God has done first is an important principle to learn. All thankfulness is a response to something God initiated, whether it is a provision, a gift, a bit of wisdom, or some spiritual grace. One could say that the Examen starts with a response on our part to something God has already provided. The provision is there, and the thankful person finds it and acknowledges it. For the person who has cultivated an attitude of gratefulness, every circumstance offers an opportunity to express thanks. In the words of James, "Every good thing given and every perfect gift is from above, coming down from the Father of lights, with whom there is no variation or shifting shadow" (James 1:17, *NASB*).

I have had the opportunity to counsel many people in my life, and one theme has emerged as a common denominator in those who are discouraged and on the edge of despair: They do not recognize the good things God has provided for them. Others can look at such a person's life and see the relationships they have, along with the blessings of a home, health, or employment, and consider them abundantly blessed. But the person who is greatly discouraged is often blind to God's goodness due to fear, rejection, or self-centeredness.

When I was a boy, I created a small business for myself by mowing lawns in the summer and clearing snow from driveways with a snow blower in the winter. Each year I would go into the garage and take my father's snow blower and set out to make some extra money. I thought I was a pretty good little businessman, very resourceful and hardworking, but in reality, there was much I took for granted. I was very fortunate that the snow blower and the lawn mower never broke, as this would have left me with no way of making money.

My little business became bigger as I contracted with neighbors to mow their lawns for five dollars and then paid my friends to mow that lawn for three, leaving me with a two-dollar profit. I truly thought I was a self-made man at the age of ten because my self-centered attitude blinded me to reality. In retrospect, I realize now that I was very blessed, but I never saw the blessing due to my myopic (nearsighted) worldview. It didn't hit me until I became an adult that I never had to check to see if the machines were filled with gas.

The gas was always there, not because I was a good manager of my resources but because the machines were always working due to my father's diligence. I don't ever recall thinking, "The reason this little business of mine is so successful is because my father provided both the machines and the fuel for my business and never even asks for recognition." My father paid the cost for me because he loved me and was thrilled with my entrepreneurial spirit. Once I realized the truth of my success, I went to my father and thanked him for not only those unrecognized gifts of machine and gas, but for many of the other gifts he gave me growing up that I did not credit him for.

There are a lot of unrecognized gifts in all of our lives, and yet we continue on as if we're the talented ones worthy of praise. Living with this attitude sets us up for great disappointment when a gift is removed or appears to fail us. If our attitude is one that recognizes the gifts placed in our lives and responds to God in thankfulness, then when things don't work out, we will continue to thank God, knowing he has plenty more blessings to bestow. When we live in thankfulness, all gifts are tied to the one we love and trust, and life becomes a celebration of God's goodness rather than a struggle to survive as one who is alone in this world.

Recognizing the various gifts from God in your life is like

exercising a muscle—the more you do it, the stronger and more efficient you become. Again, this was a lesson I learned as a boy. When I was young, my father took me out into the woods to hunt for morel mushrooms. I didn't know exactly what they looked like until my father pointed one out. Once I really learned what a morel mushroom looked like, they started to show up everywhere. I went from walking right by them to seeing them everywhere. The more mushrooms I spotted, the easier finding these well-camouflaged delicacies became. Now I see the treasures that others just pass by.

This principle is also true in the spiritual life. At first, it might seem difficult to spot blessings from God, particularly for Americans. We are taught to be independent and resourceful, a virtue that can cloud reality at times. But once we make a daily habit of spotting gifts from God, it actually becomes easier, and everything starts to present itself as a gift. A thankful heart teaches the eyes to see more clearly, to transcend the natural, and to begin to see the supernatural.

C.S. Lewis points out that hidden in the blessings of this world are hints of blessings that go beyond this world.

> All things that have ever deeply possessed you should have been but hints of [heaven]—tantalizing glimpses, promises never quite fulfilled, echoes that died away just as they caught your ear.... If I find in myself a desire which no experience in this world can satisfy, the more probable explanation is that I was made for another world.... Earthly pleasures were never meant to satisfy it, but only to arouse it, to suggest the real thing.[23]

One could say that recognition of the gifts of God in this life are but a prelude for something much better. It's like thanking God for zirconium in this life, knowing that diamonds will come in heaven.

Whether you utilize the Examen on a daily basis or not, it would be fruitful to start every day by thanking God for his blessings. Recognizing the valuable things in your life does not usually happen by accident; rather, it is the result of purposeful thinking. As Christians, we see the things of this world differently than those who do not believe in a benevolent, loving God. The world sees a rainstorm; the Christian sees nourishment. The world sees suffering and pain; the Christian sees an opportunity to love like Christ.

In order to develop this holy habit of recognizing the gifts from God in your life, start with some of the obvious gifts in your family, home, and work. You could focus on tangible items and then move to intangible things. You could thank God for the big things in your life and then take a day to thank him for the smallest things in your life. Many small things actually mean a lot, and the list is endless. The laugh of your child is very meaningful. If something were to happen to your child, you would yearn for the day when you enjoyed the gift of that joyful smile. You could focus on your physical abilities or cognitive skills such as reading, reasoning, and exercising your will. Once you get started, you'll see blessings everywhere. Isn't that a dynamic way to live?

PEOPLE OF PRAISE

The bottom line is that we as Catholics are meant to be people of praise and thanksgiving. Praise and thanksgiving marks our prayer, our worship, our words, and our deeds. Praise and thanksgiving should be the hallmark of everything in our life.

In conclusion, I would encourage you to take what you have learned from this book and start to develop habits. It is said that a habit is developed when you repeat something for at least thirty days. There is something about the repetition of good action that develops virtue in the human heart. I would challenge you to use some of these tips in both the praise and thanksgiving sections to craft a life plan. I know that if you do, your life will change for the good. Let us together join in and praise God and give him thanks, for this is what we will be doing in heaven for all eternity.

Key Takeaways

- The Examen, part of Ignatian spiritual exercises, is a beautiful prayer encounter with Christ designed to transform us.
- Gratitude is the way we acknowledge God's blessings and loving presence in our lives.
- Fear, rejection, or self-centeredness can blind us to God's goodness.
- God's blessings in this life are just a foretaste of what we will experience in eternity.

Questions for Reflection

1. How do you typically begin your day? What are the first thoughts you have or words out of your mouth?
2. Do you find it easy or challenging to list God's blessings in your life? If you find it challenging, take some time for purposeful thinking. Journal about what comes to mind as you do this.

3. At your next family meal together, go around the table and ask family members to share two things they are especially thankful for. You might want to make this a daily habit!

Ten Tips for Developing
a Thankful Heart

1. Thank God for things in your life that people often forget or overlook.
The Nobel Prizes are given out every year to people who have accomplished amazing things. In the area of science, men and women have figured out how to take common elements on earth and twist, stretch, and mix and match them into something that we hope moves humanity forward.

Great minds like Albert Einstein dwelled on the small things of life, such as atoms, light, and sound, and eventually they found themselves dealing with reactions that had big consequences. Large amounts of energy were released from relatively small amounts of matter. Many scientists didn't start with the big things; they started with little things. The kingdom of heaven is like this. Jesus said:

> With what can we compare the kingdom of God, or what parable shall we use for it? It is like a grain of mustard seed, which, when sown upon the ground, is the smallest of all the seeds on earth; yet when it is sown it grows up and becomes the greatest of all shrubs, and puts forth large branches, so that the birds of the air can make nests in its shade. (Mark 4:30–32)

Spend some time thinking about those things that others take for granted or bypass as mundane and a given in life. You just may find out that what others are missing is actually the key to something wonderful in your life. An example would be the air you breathe or the electrical charge in your heart. Think about it—without either of these you wouldn't be here!

2. Recognize that everything you have is a gift.
There are two ways of looking at life and all that you have. You can see your whole life, your possessions, accomplishments, and relationships as yours, the fruit of your genius, or you can see all of your life as a gift from God. Once you see everything as gift, it not only changes your relationship with possessions, accomplishments, and others, but thankfulness begins to well up in your heart as you acknowledge what great things God has brought into your life.

For example, at the time of this writing, I'm looking outside and enjoying a beautiful snowfall in Minnesota. The beauty around our house is a gift from God that reminds me of just how creative he is. I'm also thankful for the gift of a snowblower, because I'm going to have to remove that gift of snow from the driveway. Speaking of the driveway, that was a gift, too. Our driveway goes uphill from the street to the house, which makes getting to our home so much easier than driving through mud. Did I mention the warm clothing necessary to work outside in a Minnesota winter? That's a gift, too.

The more you acknowledge the stuff of your life as pure gift from God, the more you start to take notice. The more you credit God with, the more you see each day. If you were to develop this habit of being thankful by seeing everything as gift, the beautiful spice of thankfulness would season your day.

Take some time today and spice up your life by naming things in your life as a gift. If you find this difficult, you may want to work on the virtue of humility. Humility is the proper assessment of who you are in relationship to God and others. Go ahead and verbally express that thanks to God. This is how habits are formed.

3. Live in the present moment.
One of the beautiful skills God gave us is that we, like God, are able to experience the past, present, and future. We have this gift of "being everywhere" (to a lesser degree, of course). While this is an amazing ability, it does have its drawbacks if we don't discipline our minds. We can dwell on the past, which typically takes the form of regret and disappointment. We can also improperly dwell in the future by worrying and living in fear. Paul said,

> Brethren, I do not consider that I have made it my own; but one thing I do, forgetting what lies behind and straining forward to what lies ahead. I press on toward the goal for the prize of the upward call of God in Christ Jesus. (Philippians 3:13–14)

Solomon wrote, "He has made everything beautiful in its time; also he has put eternity into man's mind, yet so that he cannot find out what God has done from the beginning to the end" (Ecclesiastes 3:11). If you live in the present moment and concentrate on what God is doing in your life today, you will not be burdened by yesterday or worried about tomorrow. Matthew said, "Therefore do not be anxious about tomorrow, for tomorrow will be anxious for itself. Let the day's own trouble be sufficient for the day" (Matthew 6:34).

Take the trouble of today and transform it with a thankful heart. This is the formula for successful living. Share this key with your family and friends. The hope is that they will have seen it demonstrated in your life many times. Remember: If you live in yesterday or tomorrow, you will not be able to be a witness today, nor will you be able to appreciate all that you currently have. Don't miss the life in front of you by letting yesterday and tomorrow steal from you!

4. Pray it forward.

You no doubt have heard the often-quoted phrase, "pay it forward." In recent years this concept of blessing someone else without them expecting it has become very popular. When people pay it forward, it is many times an expression of gratitude for what one has and an offering to others and an opportunity to share in one's blessings.

Our life can become a living prayer, a living sacrifice of thanksgiving by giving the good gifts we have received to others. Let's call that "praying it forward"! A thankful heart is a giving heart whose life becomes a beautiful walking prayer to God. As Luke says:

> Give, and it will be given to you; good measure, pressed down, shaken together, running over, will be put into your lap. For the measure you give will be the measure you get back. (Luke 6:38)

Most people have heard the story of the feeding of the five thousand in the Gospel. The topic of thankfulness is at the heart of the story where bread and fish are multiplied and shared. Thankfulness was the key to multiplying the blessings, the gifts of God. Realizing that the feeding of the five thousand was talking about a great miracle, the Eucharist, we can better understand the central place of thanksgiving in the great exchange from bread to the body of Christ and from wine to the blood of Christ. The Eucharistic Prayer is saturated with thankfulness.

> We give thanks to you, O God, for the goodness and love which you have made known to us in creation; in the calling of Israel to be your people; in your Word spoken through the prophets; and above all in the Word made flesh, Jesus, your Son. For in these last days you sent him to be incarnate from the Virgin Mary, to be the Savior and Redeemer of the world. In him, you have delivered us from evil, and made us worthy to stand before you. In him, you have brought us out of error into truth, out of sin into righteousness, out of death into life.
>
> On the night before he died for us, our Lord Jesus Christ took bread; and when he had given thanks to you, he broke it, and gave it to his disciples, and said, "Take, eat: This is my Body, which is given for you. Do this in remembrance of me." After supper he took the cup of wine; and when he had given thanks, he gave it to them, and said, "Drink this, all of you: This is my Blood of the new Covenant, which is shed for you and for many for the forgiveness of sins. Whenever you drink it, do this for the remembrance of me."

Make *everything* in your life an opportunity to express thanks. You can do that by bringing your life to Mass and joining the supreme sacrifice of Christ. You can also make every opportunity an expression of thanks by noticing the need of others around you. Watch and see—if you do pray it forward, you're probably going to hear "Thanks!" from someone.

5. Thank God publicly and corporately.

A foundational practice of the Church is the gathering together on Sunday to remember the death of our Lord and rejoice in his resurrection. This time together is the best way to show God our thanks. As Christians, we are called to come together to strengthen one another.

> And let us consider how to stir up one another to love and good works, not neglecting to meet together, as is the habit of some, but encouraging one another, and all the more as you see the Day drawing near. (Hebrews 10:24–25)

The Mass is the primary way we offer thanksgiving corporately. The Mass is called the Eucharist, which means "thanksgiving" from the Greek word *eucharistia*. On many occasions throughout the Mass, thanks are expressed by the priest and the congregation.

- During the *Gloria* the congregation sings, "We give you thanks for your great glory."
- In the *Liturgy of the Word* the congregation responds with "Thanks be to God" after the first readings.
- The priest says in the *Eucharistic Prayer*, "Let us give thanks to the Lord our God."
- *In Eucharistic Prayer I*, the priest speaks of Jesus' actions, when he says, "The day before he suffered he took bread in his sacred hands and looking up to heaven, to you, his almighty Father, he gave you thanks and praise."
- At the end of the *Concluding Rite*, the congregation responds to the priest's "Go in peace to love and serve the lord" with a resounding "Thanks be to God."

The *Catechism of the Catholic Church* has a lot to say about thanksgiving being a major part of the corporate life of the Church. Read 2637—2649 for more on this subject. It will give you a whole new perspective of how central thanksgiving is to the life of the Church.

6. Allow the Holy Spirit to awaken your memory during the Liturgy of the Word.
According to the *Catechism*, the Holy Spirit will inspire thanksgiving and praise during Mass.

> The liturgical celebration always refers to God's saving interventions in history. "The economy of Revelation is realized by deeds and words, which are intrinsically bound up with each other.... [T]he words for their part proclaim the works and bring to light the mystery they contain." In the Liturgy of the Word, the Holy Spirit "recalls" to the assembly all that Christ has done for us. (CCC 1103)

"The Holy Spirit 'recalls' to the assembly all that Christ has done for us." That's the key, right there. That's why we say, "The Word of the Lord." And the response? "Thanks be to God." The Holy Spirit awakens the memory of the entire Church, and that in turn inspires thanksgiving.

Our response to the Word of God is "Thanks be to God." That's the Holy Spirit moving in our hearts, awakening us, along with the rest of the Church, to God's saving deeds. This is a really important point, because so often at Mass when the Word is read and saving deeds of God are proclaimed, we are checked out. Our minds are somewhere else. Five minutes after the readings, how often can you not recount anything that was said, even if your life depended on it?

The Holy Spirit is there to help us to remember, but we are just so restless, and our mind is on so many other things. We need to allow the Holy Spirit to awaken our memory during the Liturgy of the Word. We need to be awake. We need to be focused. This is all part of cultivating thanksgiving in our lives.

7. Voluntarily fast from something you take for granted.
They say that absence makes the heart grow fonder. I know that is true in relationships, but I have also come to realize just how true it is when I run out of something around the house. My wife and I drink tea every morning. I make black tea, and we enjoy a cup, along with discussion and prayer. I like my tea with a "spot" of cream, as the English say, and she prefers hers black. When I brew the tea and get ready to serve it, I go to the refrigerator and reach for the half-and-half. Some days the half-and-half is not there, leaving me less than happy. That's when I need to stop and recognize how thankful I am for something like cream, which I tend to take for granted.

Yes, it's true: Fasting from anything can make you more thankful. Give up eating for a day, and you will be very thankful for your next meal! Let that fast turn your heart into thanksgiving for the food that God has given you. You can also fast from other things you take for granted. It might be your transportation to work. Maybe instead of taking the bus tomorrow, you'll choose to walk or ride your bike. As you walk to work, thank God for your car or for the bus. Use your imagination—see if you can come up with some other ways to refrain from something you normally take for granted. You'll gain a fresh perspective and increase your praise vocabulary in the process.

The liturgical calendar gives us forty days of Lent to prepare our hearts for the Easter season; often believers will grow in Christ by fasting from something that they find a delight.

8. Keep a record of God's faithfulness to you.

In other words, count your blessings—"Name them one by one," as the old song says. There are a number of ways of doing this. You can start a tradition in your household to keep track of God's faithfulness. You can create a scrapbook as a family. You could start a website or a blog for your extended family as a way to keep track of God's faithfulness. Keep a journal by the phone and jot down news you receive from friends and relatives. Come up with your own way to keep a record of your thankfulness for God's faithful presence in your life.

In our family, for instance, every year since we have been married, we acquire a Christmas ornament that somehow expresses something that year we are remembering and are thankful for. Over the years, we are reminded of God's thankfulness in a multitude of ways.

For this year, we got a little dog ornament with Tubby's name on it to commemorate our new puppy. It reminds us of the fact that we are very thankful to God for giving us this wonderful pet. He is a rescue dog that has brought joy to every member of the family. We have ornaments commemorating the years our daughters were born, the year we built a house, our twenty-fifth wedding anniversary, and moving back to Minnesota from Alabama to be closer to our families.

One older couple I know has a really unique way of remembering what they are thankful for. Every year since they got married, they have cut an inch from the trunk of their Christmas tree. They mark these with the year and one or two things they have been especially thankful for during the past year, and then they string these together and display this decoration every year. Now this couple has been married for over fifty years, and every year when they put up the ornaments, all their grandkids and great-grandkids can read about years of thanksgiving to God. They might even find themselves there, that back in 1969 their grandparents were thankful when they were born.

This is a good example of being creative. You can come up with your own family traditions, your own ways of recording God's faithfulness to you so you can give him thanks.

9. Show gratitude and thankfulness toward others.
There are lots of ways to do this, but it's amazing how easy it is to forget and just take each other for granted. Here's one way: Think of three people who have had an impact on your life and write each of them a thank-you note. Paul told the Corinthians that generosity is not only supplying the needs of God's people, but it also overflows in many expressions of thanks to God (see 2 Corinthians 9:11–12). In other words, Paul equated being generous toward others with thanksgiving to God. The *Catechism* has something to say about this, too. It tells us to thank those who have passed on the faith to us.

> For Christians a special gratitude is due to those from whom they have received the gift of faith, the grace of baptism, and life in the Church. These may include parents, grandparents, other members of the family, pastors, catechists, and other teachers or friends (CCC 2220).

Who in your life was responsible for passing on the faith to you? For most of us, it was our parents, grandparents, and godparents. But think about others who impacted you. Who was your CCD teacher? Your confirmation instructor? Was there a particular priest or nun? Maybe there were aunts and uncles who taught you about the faith. If they are still alive, express your thanks in writing.

Expressing your thanks to God for those who passed on the faith to you might include showing your gratitude in even more tangible ways. Part of showing respect for your parents includes showing your gratitude by taking care of them in their old age. The *Catechism* says that is a form of thanksgiving (see CCC 2215). This is an example of how a horizontal expression results in a vertical display of thanksgiving. Our vertical demonstration of thanks to God is expressed by what we do horizontally, as far as thanking and taking care of people—especially thanking those who passed on the faith to us. The *Catechism* says that Jesus called this the "duty of gratitude" (see CCC 2218).

This year, my mother-in-law is celebrating her eightieth birthday, and this gave my wife and I pause to think about her life and her influence upon us. As we look back on the many testimonies we have received from people who were blessed by a book or talk we have done, it really extends back to my mother-in-law, Alice Tobler, a woman who has been incredibly generous with her time in the area of passing on the faith. She spent many hours talking about the Bible with me as a young man, and she influenced my wife in a huge way to love Jesus and live for him every day. I would be remiss if I didn't thank her for all she did to support us through the years with encouragement and prayers. In her honor, we are having a big party to celebrate her life. For anyone out there who has been impacted in any way through me or my wife, you have Alice to thank.

Another person in my life for whom I am very grateful is Mr. Knight, my English teacher. I have a confession. When I was growing up, I didn't consider myself too bright. I was very bad at English, writing, public speaking—these were huge areas of weakness for me. In the sixth grade, I had a great teacher named Mr. Knight. One of the things that made him great was that every day he would gather the class around him, and he would read chapters of epic adventures, the great classics, to us. While some of the kids were restless and resorted to goofing off, I was captivated. One book that particularly enthralled me was *Robinson Crusoe*. I sat there listening every day to Mr. Knight and the way he read it, and the passion that he had was contagious.

At that point, I became somewhat addicted to adventure. I started reading other adventure books: *My Side of the Mountain, Swiss Family Robinson, Last of the Mohicans*, and *Moby-Dick*.

One day Mr. Knight gave us the assignment to write a five-page story. Mr. Knight had so inspired me that I went home and wrote a 168-page story—without a single bit of punctuation. I turned my assignment in, and Mr. Knight got a chuckle out of it. When he met with my parents at the next parent-teacher conference, he said, "Well, one thing is for sure, he has a big imagination and he likes adventure, but he is not a good writer in terms of punctuation." That started me on my love for books. From that year on, I could not stop reading. In the summer I would mow lawns, and in the winter I would shovel driveways, just to get enough money to buy books—and then I would read, read, read! I have to thank Mr. Knight for that.

In 2000, my first book, *My Life on the Rock*, was published. It was an autobiography, telling the story of my conversion. When I traveled from Alabama to Minneapolis to visit family, I brought several copies with me. One of the copies I planned to give Mr. Knight. I went back to my old elementary school and discovered he was no longer teaching there. They told me that he was at a school across the city, so I drove there just to see if I could catch him by chance. I went to the principal's office, and they told me what room he was in. I walked in and saw this older man—far, far older than when I was a sixth-grade boy. He looked at me as though he recognized me. Just to be sure, I told him, "I'm Jeff Cavins."

"I remember," he said, "the boy who wrote the long story."

Looking at him, I had to fight back my emotions. I told him, "Mr. Knight, I've written my first book, and it's just been published. I just wanted to come back and thank you for giving me a love for books."

His eyes began to water, and he said, "I've never had a student come back like this." I thought, *What a pity that we do not go back and thank the people that changed our lives.*

So here's my challenge to you. Think about those who have impacted your life and give thanks for them. Find a way to express that gratitude to them.

10. If you are suffering from anxiety or worry, begin cultivating a life of thanksgiving.

Paul commanded the Philippians to cultivate a life of thanksgiving:

> Have no anxiety about anything, but in everything
> by prayer and supplication with thanksgiving let your

requests be made known to God. And the peace of God, which passes all understanding, will keep your hearts and your minds in Christ Jesus. (Philippians 4:6–7)

If you are filled with anxiety, cultivate a life of thanksgiving. As you begin to pray and petition God, no matter how anxious you feel, make sure to pepper your prayers with praise and thanksgiving. The result will be the peace that passes understanding, just like the Bible promises.

Many people these days suffer from insomnia. Are you one of them? The Bible offers an antidote. Psalm 119:62 says, "At midnight I rise to praise thee." People do all kinds of things when they cannot sleep, from watching TV in the middle of the night or reading books to wandering around the house. The psalmist says that, if you are restless at night, get up and give thanks to God. Often you cannot sleep because there is a burden you are carrying that is really meant to be given to God. So, the next time you are plagued with a sleepless night, try giving thanks to God instead of some other remedy found on late night TV.

Appendix A

What the *Catechism of the Catholic Church* Says about Praise and Thanksgiving

2649 Prayer of praise is entirely disinterested and rises to God, lauds him, and gives him glory for his own sake, quite beyond what he has done, but simply because HE IS (see also 2639–2641).

2637 Thanksgiving characterizes the prayer of the Church which, in celebrating the Eucharist, reveals and becomes more fully what she is. Indeed, in the work of salvation, Christ sets creation free from sin and death to consecrate it anew and make it return to the Father, for his glory. The thanksgiving of the members of the Body participates in that of their Head.

2638 As in the prayer of petition, every event and need can become an offering of thanksgiving. The letters of St. Paul often begin and end with thanksgiving, and the Lord Jesus is always present in it: "Give thanks in all circumstances; for this is the will of God in Christ Jesus for you"; "Continue steadfastly in prayer, being watchful in it with thanksgiving."

2642 The prophets and the saints, all those who were slain on earth for their witness to Jesus, the vast throng of those who, having come through the great tribulation, have gone before us into the Kingdom, all sing the praise and glory of him who sits on the throne, and of the Lamb. In communion with them, the Church on earth also sings these songs with faith in the midst of trial. By means of petition and intercession faith hopes against all hope and gives thanks to the "Father of lights,"... Thus faith is pure praise.

2648   Every joy and suffering, every event and need can become the matter for thanksgiving which, sharing in that of Christ, should fill one's whole life: "Give thanks in all circumstances" (1 *Thess* 5:18).

2643   The Eucharist contains and expresses all forms of prayer; it is...*the* "sacrifice of praise."

1103   In the Liturgy of the Word the Holy Spirit "recalls" to the assembly all that Christ has done for us.... The Holy Spirit who thus awakens the memory of the Church then inspires thanksgiving and praise.

Appendix B

Fifty Bible Verses on Praise

1. Exodus 15:2
2. Judges 5:3
3. 2 Samuel 22:4, 50
4. 1 Chronicles 16:9, 25, 34–36
5. 1 Chronicles 29:13
6. 2 Chronicles 5:13–14
7. 2 Chronicles 7:3
8. Ezra 3:11
9. Nehemiah 9:5
10. Psalm 2:11
11. Psalm 7:17
12. Psalm 9:2, 11
13. Psalm 18:3, 49
14. Psalm 21:13
15. Psalm 30:4, 11–12
16. Psalm 34:1–3
17. Psalm 35:28
18. Psalm 40:3
19. Psalm 42:5, 11
20. Psalm 48:1
21. Psalm 51:15
22. Psalm 56:4
23. Psalm 57:7
24. Psalm 63:3, 5
25. Psalm 69:30, 34

26. Psalm 71:5–6, 8, 14
27. Psalm 74:21
28. Psalm 78:4
29. Psalm 79:13
30. Psalm 96:4
31. Psalm 100:4
32. Psalm 108:1, 3
33. Psalm 109:30
34. Psalm 113:1, 3
35. Psalm 145:21
36. Psalm 150:1–6
37. Isaiah 25:1
38. Isaiah 43:21
39. Jeremiah 20:13
40. Daniel 2:23
41. Joel 2:26
42. Luke 19:37–38
43. Acts 16:25–26
44. Romans 14:11
45. Romans 15:8–10
46. Ephesians 1:3
47. Hebrews 13:15
48. James 5:13
49. Revelation 7:12
50. Revelation 19:5–6

Appendix C

Fifty Bible Verses on Thanksgiving

1. 1 Chronicles 16:8, 34
2. 1 Chronicles 23:30
3. 1 Chronicles 29:13
4. Psalm 7:17
5. Psalm 28:7
6. Psalm 34:1
7. Psalm 35:18
8. Psalm 50:14
9. Psalm 69:30
10. Psalm 75:1
11. Psalm 95:2–3
12. Psalm 100:4
13. Psalm 106:1
14. Psalm 107:8
15. Psalm 111:1
16. Psalm 118:28
17. Psalm 136:1
18. Psalm 138:1
19. Psalm 147:7
20. Isaiah 12:4
21. Jeremiah 33:11
22. Jonah 2:9
23. Matthew 26:27
24. Mark 6:41
25. Luke 17:11–19

26. John 11:41
27. Romans 1:21
28. Romans 16:4
29. 1 Corinthians 1:4
30. 1 Corinthians 10:16
31. 1 Corinthians 15:57
32. 2 Corinthians 2:14
33. 2 Corinthians 4:15–16
34. 2 Corinthians 9:11
35. Ephesians 1:15–16
36. Ephesians 5:4
37. Ephesians 5:19–21
38. Philippians 1:3
39. Philippians 4:6
40. Colossians 2:7
41. Colossians 3:15, 17
42. Colossians 4:2
43. 1 Thessalonians 1:2
44. 1 Thessalonians 5:18
45. 1 Timothy 4:4–5
46. 1 Timothy 2:1
47. 1 Timothy 4:4
48. Hebrews 12:28–29
49. James 5:13
50. Revelation 11:17

NOTES

1. See "Prayer of Saint Teresa of Avila," *EWTN*, http://www. ewtn.com/devotionals/prayers/stteresaofavila.htm.
2. Quoting 2 Corinthians 6:18; see Matthew 6:32.
3. Quoting St. Thomas Aquinas, *STh* I, 25, 5, *ad* 1.
4. Charles H. Spurgeon, *Sermons of Rev. C.H. Spurgeon of London* (New York: Funk & Wagnalls, 1976), p. 357.
5. Quoted in Charlie Jones and Bob Kelly, eds., *The Tremendous Power of Prayer* (West Monroe, La.: Howard, 2000), p. 112.
6. Pope Benedict XVI, General Audience, November 14, 2012.
7. Quoting 1 Corinthians 4:7; Psalm 166:42.
8. See Lawrence J. Epstein, "Spirituality: Search and Recovery," *Beliefnet*, http://www.beliefnet.com/Faiths/ Spirituality-Search-and-Recovery.aspx.
9. See Margaret Wheeler Johnson, "Adrianne Haslet-Davis, Dance Teacher Who Lost Foot In Boston Bombing, Has Amazingly Positive Outlook (VIDEO)," *The Huffington Post*, April 23, 2013, http://www.huffingtonpost. com/2013/04/23/adrianne-haslet-davis-lost-foot-boston-bombing_n_3142067.html.
10. See Stephen Hawking's bio at his official website, http:// www.hawking.org.uk/index.html.
11. Homily VIII, available at http://www.tertullian.org/fathers2/ NPNF1-13/npnf1-13-57.htm.
12. *The End*, directed by Burt Reynolds (Gordon-Reynolds Productions, 1978).

13. Dr. Tim Gray, *Catholic for a Reason III: Scripture and the Mystery of the Mass* (Steubenville, Ohio: Emmaus Road, 2004), pp. 70–71.
14. St. Justin Martyr, *Apologia*, bk. 1, chap. 65, in *Ante-Nicene Fathers*, vol 1.
15. Dr. Tim Gray, *Catholic for a Reason III*, p. 74.
16. Taken from the Pesiqta as quoted in Hartmut Gese, *Essays on Biblical Theology* (Minneapolis: Augsburg, 1981), p. 133.
17. Citing Paul VI, *MF*, 66.
18. Daria Sockey, *The Everyday Catholic's Guide to the Liturgy of the Hours* (Cincinnati: Servant, 2013), p. 17.
19. Taken from the prayer for the preparation of the Easter Candle from the Easter Vigil.
20. *The Spiritual Exercises of St. Ignatius*, trans. Father Elder Mullan, S.J., 43, http://www.jesuit.org/jesuits/wp-content/uploads/The-Spiritual-Exercises-.pdf.
21. Timothy M. Gallagher, *The Examen Prayer: Ignatian Wisdom for Our Lives Today* (New York: Crossroad, 2006), pp. 58–59.
22. Gallagher, *The Examen Prayer*, p. 59.
23. [need additional source]
24. C.S. Lewis, *Mere Christianity* (San Francisco: Harper Collins, 2001), pp. 136–137.

About the Author

Jeff Cavins is director of evangelization for the Archdiocese of Saint Paul and Minneapolis, the creator of the popular Great Adventure Bible Study series and the founding host of EWTN's weekly program *Life on the Rock*. He is an international speaker and the author of several books, including *Walking with God: A Journey through the Bible*. He and his wife, Emily, lead annual pilgrimages to the Holy Land.